COUNT ME PRESENT

COMBATING THE TRUANCY EPIDEMIC

A Critical Review of Truancy Within Our Public School Systems

AUTHOR

SUSIE WINFIELD

INTRODUCTION

This book is a tribute to the dedication of all school administrators, teachers, counselors, office personnel, and stakeholders who invest daily in the lives of our children. Our role is crucial and invaluable in understanding and addressing the myriad of challenges our children face. This book will raise awareness about truancy and attendance issues. Active participation will make a significant difference. It offers actionable strategies and a step-by-step guide for school administrators and stakeholders to enhance practical effectiveness. These theoretical and practical strategies can be applied in any school setting or district. Readers will understand how to promote clear pathways to implementing change by raising awareness of the issues plaguing our students in school. Bringing awareness will teach us to reflect on the various problems surrounding our children's daily attendance, highlighting the issues and ultimately fostering a sense of empowerment and collaboration that will help make the necessary changes to promote accountability within our schools and school districts. There are surveys herein that will enhance and create a more open dialogue between home and school.

The interventions and scenarios outlined in this book will illuminate the many underlying factors contributing to our children's school absenteeism. Our primary aim is to educate and raise awareness about school absences and truancy. The challenges our children face daily are significant. This resource aims to provide support and insight to foster the educational growth of families and children by positively influencing their behaviors. Additionally, this resource will empower schools to actively promote change by shifting students' and their families' mindsets regarding the critical importance of school attendance accountability. Each intervention presented is grounded in factual evidence. To uphold the privacy and integrity of the families involved, I've taken steps to alter their names in these examples.

I hope you find this information valuable and that it helps enhance classroom and school attendance, ultimately improving attendance standards across school districts. The practical strategies offered are easy to integrate into your daily routines, making this book a valuable resource in your efforts to promote attendance and engagement.

All the interventions presented in this book were gathered during my experience working in various school districts. Throughout this journey, I sought divine guidance as I served our children and families, recognizing the need for deeper insights into the challenges of children's daily attendance. Fortunately, these prayers were answered. You may wonder why divine guidance is essential regarding children's attendance. Every community has two vital pillars: the church and the school. These institutions play a crucial role in shaping our character and instilling accountability from a young age. We must approach our interactions within these sacred spaces with love, respect, and a deep understanding to create meaningful change.

We must be intentional and strategic about the changes we wish to see, working collaboratively to ensure our children receive the support they need to thrive. In our commitment to serving humanity, developing strong listening skills is essential to gathering the information needed to support our children's success. I must admit this work is often challenging. However, identifying and implementing strategic methods can foster the change we wish to see in our schools. Initiatives such as early intervention programs and cultivating a supportive school culture are critical.

Most importantly, these approaches encourage our children to recognize the significance of attending school. One of the key lessons I've learned is that truancy is not merely a problem confined to schools or families; it's a pressing community issue. It calls for collaboration among all stakeholders to improve our children's well-being. By joining forces, we can create an environment that promotes attendance and supports the holistic development of every student.

I have dedicated many hours to researching truancy behaviors across various school districts, and through my findings, I've identified numerous factors that contribute to truancy and poor attendance. If you work in a school, you're likely familiar with how these factors often fall into at least one of the following categories: family dynamics, school culture, community influences, and individual student variables. Throughout this book, we will explore these underlying factors in greater detail. While analyzing attendance and behavioral data from different school districts, I discovered a concerning trend: many parents keep their children at home until after Labor Day. The reasons for this enrollment delay remain unclear. We will also explore the necessary changes within school cultures to promote our children's growth and success. By understanding these dynamics, we can strive to create a supportive environment that fosters consistent attendance and engagement in the educational process.

Our school environments must adopt a strategic approach to addressing various issues. By establishing the necessary standards, we can help our children overcome challenges and develop into productive individuals. These issues undoubtedly affect both school attendance and behavior. The scope of this work, however, is to improve attendance through proven strategies and methods. This begins with being intentional as we modify the antiquated attendance standards in many school districts across the nation. If we want change, we must raise the standard; the higher the standard, the more parents and students will comply. This change is not just possible; it is within our reach, and it begins with each one of us being intentional about the change we want to see in our children's school experience.

How can we advocate for our children's success? We fight by improving the standards that reflect the challenges of our day. We call on everyone in the school system with the knowledge, ability, and understanding to implement the needed standards to increase attendance. We recognize and appreciate the efforts that have already been made. We know that we can make a significant difference with your continued support. We can no longer assume that things will change in our schools unless we first adopt the standards that will enable our children and parents to thrive.

"Count Me Present" is a powerful call to action. It represents our commitment to enhancing school attendance and emphasizes the need for daily accountability from our children and families. I hope you, the reader, will find the interventions and topics within these pages valuable and inspiring. We have the opportunity to initiate a movement focused on accountability, one that can lead to more children being present in our classrooms each day. As lifelong learners, we continually explore new ideas to transform the dynamics within our schools, ensuring that every stakeholder benefits. Let us strive for a future where every child is eager to participate and succeed in their educational journey.

I can envision our children joyfully exclaiming, "Count Me Present!" I hope that this grows into a nationwide movement that directly addresses truancy. But how do we make this a reality? It begins with implementing changes to our existing standards and fostering a culture where our children's voices are valued and heard. By echoing their enthusiasm, raising our hands, and confidently declaring, "Count Me Present," we can lay the groundwork for a brighter future centered around consistent attendance and engagement in education. Let's create an environment where every child feels valued and committed to showing up daily. Let's kick off the "Count Me Present" movement! Are you ready to raise your hands in solidarity with our students? It's time to change our school culture by being strategic and intentional in our attendance approach. Together, we can make a difference and commit to every child's educational journey. Let's unite and take action—Count Me Present!

TABLE OF CONTENTS

Foreword

My mother, Susie Winfield, has never been one for empty words. Her life serves as a testament to action, service, and an unwavering belief in the importance of showing up. As an Army veteran, a retired police officer, and a former school truancy liaison, she has worn the uniforms of a nation, a community, and its most vulnerable children. At home, she was "Mom"—the woman who held my siblings, Taylor, Tara, and Jaret, and me to the same high standards she later used to uplift thousands of students across various school districts. She taught us the meaning of being industrious not just through her words, but through her relentless example. We witnessed her pour the same disciplined commitment she learned in the military into ensuring that kids, who might otherwise be overlooked, made it to school and walked across the graduation stage. She wasn't just doing a job; she was on a mission. Her most powerful tool wasn't authority—it was trust.

I witnessed this firsthand. My mother implemented effective strategies to reduce truancy, but only because of the open, strategic communication she developed with students and their families. She understood that a rule without a relationship only leads to rebellion. In every interaction, she approached homes and conversations with the heart of a public servant who believed in the potential of every child and the strength of every family.

That is why this book is so essential, and I am honored to introduce it.

What you hold in your hands is more than just a theory; it's a playbook. It transforms my mother's relentless pursuit into fundamental, actionable strategies. However, it does something even more significant. It recognizes that truancy isn't merely a disciplinary issue; it's a symptom. It signals a cry for help, a sign of being overwhelmed, a barrier created by mental health struggles, fractured family lives, and a loss of hope.

Readers should engage with this book because it delivers a much-needed outcome: genuine behavior modification. It provides clear guidance on how to build a bridge of trust with disenfranchised students, communicate in ways that empower rather than alienate, and recognize the individual behind the truancy record, helping them envision a brighter future.

My mother's legacy goes beyond the uniforms she wore; it resides in the lives she transformed and the family she nurtured. This book extends that legacy. It serves as a practical, compassionate, and strategic guide for anyone determined to support a child. It is in every respect a reflection of Susie Winfield—a call to action rooted in love, strategy, and an unwavering belief that simply showing up is the first step toward making a difference.

With immense pride,

Jeremy Jarmon

Chapter 1

School Culture

Throughout my career in various school districts, I have frequently been asked by principals to evaluate the culture of their schools. While each school's culture is unique, several common factors contribute to the atmosphere. These factors include the student population, community policies, and the attitudes and values present within the school. Additionally, school culture encompasses administrators, teachers, staff, students, parents, the surrounding community, and local partners.

One of the best ways to understand a school's culture is to visit during arrival and dismissal times. These times reveal a school's orderliness, students' eagerness to enter, and whether administrators may need to make structural changes. They also reveal whether the school staff properly greets the children in the morning. If not, why not? How many staff members know most of the students by name? One parent told me that her son's administrator knew all the students by name within the school. She shared that the administrator also knew all of the students' birthdays. The administrator connected with those students, and they connected with her. We can build a better rapport with others by learning something special about them. Such as, but not limited to, the student's favorite color, pet, movie genre, or sports team.

Understanding school culture is crucial for deciphering the messages embedded in the school environment and how they shape it. This understanding is essential for devising effective strategies to reduce student tardiness. Moreover, it guides schools in better engaging with parents to improve attendance and address tardiness issues. Exploring the long-term effects of a negative school culture on student learning and development further underscores the importance of this understanding.

Tardiness is a significant factor influencing whether a school environment thrives or struggles. How many students arrive after the late bell rings without an adult to check them in? Does the percentage of tardy students on any given day exceed 5% of the student population? If so, what existing measures need to be reassessed to help reduce the number of tardy students? Consider a school with a student population of 600. If 30 or more students are tardy each day, it's essential to address this issue promptly. Are administrators or designated staff members meeting with the parents of those students who are tardy to discuss possible interventions? Is the list of tardy students consistently the same? If a child is tardy at least once each week, do they live within the district? Understanding the reasons behind excessive tardiness is crucial. We need to engage with parents or guardians to explore solutions together. We will only find effective remedies through these critical conversations, which foster transparency and support our students' growth. Failure to address tardiness will lead to a culture that does not perform at its best. Additionally, if the tardiness rate does not improve, those students will eventually become chronically absent. Remember, repeated tardiness will lead to truancy.

Another issue impacting our school culture is how administrators manage parental access to the school building. Are school administrators allowing parents to walk their children to their classrooms? If the answer is "yes," we must ask why. Allowing parents to navigate the school disrupts teachers and interferes with the school culture and climate. If the answer is "no," I commend administrators for respecting teachers' space. The beginning of each day is crucial for teachers, and it is essential that they have the opportunity to set the tone for their classrooms as students arrive. We know that some parents may accompany their child to class and wish to discuss matters related to their child with the teacher. The start of the school day is not the appropriate time for these conversations. A school's culture should be rooted in respect, discipline, and accountability.

Additionally, this understanding should extend to parents, students, and staff alike. Leadership should ensure that students do not enter the schools and disrupt classrooms throughout the day. Implementing clear standards will help address issues such as tardiness, and school leaders must ensure they are consistently enforced to foster a thriving school culture.

I enjoy reading articles and books about school culture, attendance, and behaviors that can hinder our school environment. There was an article written in 2020 by Gordana S. titled "The Ultimate Guide to Shaping School Culture." The author discusses how the school's culture shapes everything that happens there. The author discusses how school culture influences students' perceptions of attending classes and their potential for learning and growth within that environment. Teachers' and other staff members' perceptions of their work and development depend on the environment. The author notes that everything revolves around the individuals running the school.

Several factors influence our school environment, shaping a positive or negative school culture. A positive school culture recognizes and rewards students for their achievements. However, it's crucial not to wait until the end of the school year to celebrate our children's accomplishments. Instead, we should recognize their successes throughout the year. A thriving school culture is essential in creating an environment where students are motivated to set meaningful goals that promote their personal and academic growth. It is necessary to foster a supportive environment that encourages students to strive for excellence. When a child consistently misses school, we must delve deeper and understand the underlying reasons for their absence, ensuring we provide the necessary support and resources to help them re-engage in their education. Addressing any concerning behavior promptly, rather than waiting until it becomes unmanageable, is key. Early intervention is crucial in preventing escalating issues and maintaining a positive school culture.

The principal's role in shaping the school culture is paramount. As Gordana (2020) points out, the principal needs to play a 'bifocal role' to manage day-to-day school operations while also serving as a symbolic leader. This bifocal approach allows the principal to promptly address behaviors or outcomes that could compromise the school culture, reinforcing the principal's influence in shaping the school.

School leaders have an excellent opportunity to positively impact our students and staff. Addressing challenges promptly can enhance our school culture. District leaders should consider providing quarterly staff training to support daily attendance and ensure staff have the necessary resources to thrive. Additionally, gathering insights through quarterly surveys for parents and guardians will be a great way to foster engagement and build a supportive community.

Establishing clear rules to uphold our standards is crucial for maintaining a vibrant school atmosphere. It's exciting to think about how regular feedback from parents and guardians, collected through simple surveys, will help us identify areas for improvement. This proactive approach streamlines communication and shows that we truly value their input. Focusing on these initiatives can create an environment where everyone feels heard, supported, and motivated to contribute to our school's success!

A virtual parent meeting is just as valuable as an in-person one. The information we want to share remains the same, regardless of the platform we use. We do not need to alter our agenda concerning accountability measures. We need to change the standards that limit our children's growth.

I had the opportunity to learn about the Check & Connect Model years ago, a model with which many school districts are familiar. When a school implements an intervention to support a student's growth, it aligns with the principles of the Check & Connect Model. Why are interventions, check-ins, and connections important? They are vital because they help us build relationships with students and their families, fostering a shift in mindset toward better outcomes for our school environment. Our children and their families are significant to us. To provide outstanding support, we must find solutions that give our students and parents a voice and a choice in addressing the behaviors we wish to change.

I want to clarify that the safest and most sacred place for our students during weekdays is at school. Have you noticed the number of school-aged children frequenting grocery stores, retail shops, and hair salons during school hours? It's unacceptable to see so many students outside school when they should be learning. We must urgently change student attendance standards to foster a healthier school culture. I came across a shocking statistic a few years ago: on any given school day, at least 200,000 students are absent from schools across the United States. This situation demands our immediate attention and action. If accurate, we have a large city composed of unsupervised school-aged children.

As the Attendance Specialist, I collaborated with our police department to assist me during school hours. I provided each of the 32 schools assigned to me with a memo that was sent home with every student. The memo stated, "Breaking News!" It informed parents that any student in the community without adult supervision during school hours would receive a juvenile summons. As a result, we observed a significant decline in unsupervised students during school hours. I can guarantee readers that our parents will comply if you change the standards surrounding our children's daily attendance. Yes, you will encounter some resistance for several weeks, but over time, it will resolve. It is important to communicate clear expectations to the school's staff when implementing higher standards to avoid any initial pushback. All staff members must work together toward a common goal.

Every team member is valuable. Changing the culture within a school requires everyone to work together.

Let's consider an example of the significant impact of higher standards on a school culture. At a high school with an alarmingly high tardiness rate, I initiated a conversation with the principal about implementing stricter standards. I clarified that, although the situation might worsen before it improves, it was a necessary step. The principal needed to trust the process. Ultimately, he agreed and told the teachers they would no longer allow students into their classrooms after the late bell rang. Tardy students were directed to my office to secure a permission slip to enter the classroom.

On the first day, approximately 75 students were tardy. On the second day, that number increased to roughly 100 students who were tardy. Over the next few days, the numbers continued to grow. Understandably, the principal became frantic. Again, I reminded him to trust me because I knew the students were telling each other to participate in being tardy for class. They were hoping I would get tired of writing admission slips. I sent a letter to all parents informing them that students who are excessively tardy will receive an overnight suspension.

Additionally, parents would need to meet with me to implement an intervention if the tardiness continued. I defined "habitually tardy" as a student being tardy at least once every week or several times per month. The parents would need to come to the school to check their children in for class and meet with me to discuss the issue. It took students and parents about two weeks to comply with these new policies. In the mornings, I received calls from parents reporting their children's lateness on various days. Our school culture must foster accountability at all levels. It is not enough for the students to comply; all stakeholders must also be involved.

When implementing a system to change behavior, consistency is crucial for effectiveness. Although my fingers were tired from writing permission slips, I communicated the message to our students and parents, assuring them that they could not enter our school building at any time of day without facing consequences. During the process of implementing targeted interventions to address student tardiness, I engaged with a significant number of parents who consistently expressed that their children's morning delays lacked any legitimate justification. A considerable portion of these students relied on school transportation, either as bus riders or in private cars, yet many still experienced chronic lateness. The situation surrounding parents coming to the school to clear overnight suspensions understandably led to heightened frustration, as they were forced to adjust their work schedules, often sacrificing valuable time and productivity because of their children's behavior.

Recognizing the need for accountability, I facilitated a collaborative meeting where both parents and students could come together. In this discussion, we collectively signed a formal agreement, or contract, outlining the commitment to eliminate tardiness. This agreement served as an essential foundation for change, fostering a sense of shared responsibility. Throughout this process, the students realized that their parents were being held accountable for an issue stemming from their own choices and actions. This newfound awareness helped to shift perspectives and encouraged a culture of punctuality and accountability within the family unit.

It's important to understand that our students and parents should not set the standards within our schools. The cultural foundations of our educational system should prioritize high standards to ensure that both our children and parents will be productive and accountable. If these standards are not upheld, administrators may notice a decline in attendance and behavioral outcomes. We must recognize that when attendance and behavior data are low, implementing interventions to raise these standards becomes essential. Interventions are necessary for achieving improvement.

Another issue affecting our school culture is how administrators perceive students' daily attendance. Is the percentage of absent students at your school more than 3% each day? Which day of the week sees the highest number of absentees? Understanding which days experience the most absenteeism is essential, as it helps you plan events strategically on days with lower attendance rates, potentially reducing overall absenteeism.

I have worked in school districts that prefer not to use "truant" to describe students with attendance issues. To me, a truant student needs guidance due to poor attendance. This student requires some form of intervention before their situation deteriorates further. I believe that, without proper support in a school environment, a truant student, due to their vulnerability, may eventually be classified as a school dropout without intervention. A dropout is a student in grades 1 through 12 whose name has been removed from the school's rolls for reasons other than death or extended illness and who has not transferred to another public or private school. It is important to note that a student under 7 can also be classified as a dropout. We can no longer remain silent and assume that truant behavior will change on its own. We must be proactive and develop a strategic plan of action immediately.

If I were invited to your school to conduct a culture assessment, what would I find that you already know is hindering your school culture? How can we foster transparency to allow our students and parents to thrive? We must be strategic and consistent in implementing the cultural changes needed within our schools. Being strategic and consistent starts with accountability. The following chapters will enable us to explore various approaches and interventions that promote change and facilitate the necessary adjustments for a thriving school culture.

Chapter 2

Extracurricular Intervention

During my first assignment, I began working at a middle school in the same area where I had previously patrolled the streets as a law enforcement officer. The principal asked for my assistance in improving attendance. Although I had never worked in a school, I thought it would be easy; however, I quickly realized it was much more challenging than I had anticipated. I remember coming home one day and crying so hard that I had to hold onto a wall to keep from falling. Before accepting the assignment, I sought guidance through prayer; however, I was unprepared for the significant challenges that arose from limited resources. Like many schools in urban districts, securing the necessary resources can be challenging due to limited funding.

Have you ever wanted to make a positive difference in the world but struggled due to a lack of experience or knowledge? I can relate to that feeling, especially when working in schools. At that time, I was eager to help and make an impact. Still, I quickly realized that gaining the knowledge and skills necessary to overcome the challenges ahead would require considerable humility and sacrifice.

I connected with the girls at school and earned their trust, giving me a voice. As I listened to them, many expressed an interest in becoming cheerleaders. I realized that if we want our children to engage in something, we must listen to their desires and motivations. Although I understood that cheerleading wouldn't necessarily address issues like truancy, it could serve as an opportunity to bond with the female students. I enthusiastically sought approval from our leadership team. I began holding tryouts and would give the girls' names to the teachers of those interested in joining the cheerleading team. Some of the girls had behavioral issues, which would exempt them from participating in extracurricular activities. Providing the girls' names to the teachers enabled them to give me feedback about each student. This ensured that everyone had a voice in the process. Some teachers indicated that certain girls should not be part of the team due to their behavior, while others expressed concerns about the daily attendance of some girls. I needed to build trust with the teachers and strategically find a solution that would benefit all stakeholders. I informed the teachers that we would implement an intervention for girls facing attendance or behavior issues. This approach allowed teachers to feel their opinions were valued and ensured students would be held accountable for their actions. I realized my goal was to improve attendance standards and, more importantly, change the school environment. To change the school environment, it was essential to help the girls understand the importance of attending school and implementing accountability measures.

I had more girls to try out for the cheerleading team than I expected. I expected around 40 girls to join us, so you can imagine my delight when over 75 arrived! This incredible turnout presented a challenge, making me realize the importance of strategically and thoughtfully selecting our squad. When it was time to finalize the team roster, I considered how devastating it would be for the girls who did not make the team. Given the limited roster size, cutting girls from the cheerleading team was difficult. Every athlete brought unique talent and spirit, making it a challenging choice to ensure the team's success while fostering an inclusive environment. What struck me was the compelling idea of choosing all the girls. After considering including everyone, I realized we could have two teams: a basketball team and a football team. I noticed that we could involve all the girls differently during home games. Some could cheer in uniform from the sidelines, others could cheer from the bleachers, and a third group could form a dance squad.

After successfully addressing the challenge of ensuring all the girls could participate, we encountered another issue: a shortage of uniforms. I was fortunate to find a wonderful woman who donated her time and materials to make 40 uniforms—20 for the cheer squad and 20 for the dance team. The girls faced essential needs that required attention, and dedicated school staff stepped up to ensure that every aspect of the team's requirements was effectively addressed. You might wonder how forming a cheerleading squad and a dance team relates to attendance. When the girls were accepted onto the team, they were informed of an essential requirement: they had to attend school every day to participate in practices and learn the cheer routines and dance moves.

I started maintaining a roster that tracked each girl's daily attendance, behavior, and report card information. When a teacher notified me of a behavioral issue that needed attention, I would meet with the girl to discuss it. I implemented an intervention with any team member to address the underlying behavior. Moreover, the girls were not permitted to cheer until the problems had been addressed.

The attendance rate among this group of female students increased significantly, thereby improving school-wide attendance. With a student population of approximately 325, nearly 80 girls, or 25%, participate. This is a significant milestone as we strive to transform the school's culture. Furthermore, these girls' academic performance and conduct began to improve. What was happening? Namely, they had someone holding them accountable on all levels. I also built a strong rapport with the parents, allowing me to discuss, as needed, the importance of their child's daily attendance and behavioral outcomes.

This group of girls blossomed, with the majority learning to recognize the importance of accountability on all levels. Due to the size of the group, the school data underwent significant changes as well. The number was greater than 25% because when you began changing the behavior of one student in a household, you affected the entire family. Those students who had siblings, even though they were not part of the cheering group, also made great strides. The accountability process was designed to be transparent and accessible to every school-age family member, ensuring that all involved clearly understood their roles and responsibilities. I remained dedicated to this group of girls until the last sixth-graders graduated. I found myself challenged but making a significant difference in the school environment.

I was genuinely intrigued by the daily accountability required in my role. Fostering a culture of accountability is essential when working with students, particularly in a classroom setting. Keeping a student sidelined from a game wasn't a challenge stemming from behavior; instead, being part of a team created a meaningful goal for them and deepened their understanding of their responsibilities to their peers. Seeing them grow and embrace their roles within the group was rewarding!

Our students absorb values from the critical adults, including teachers, coaches, and mentors. When we overlook tardiness or absences, we unintentionally send the message that such behavior is acceptable. For instance, if a student is absent, I make a point of saying, "We missed you" to the group the following day. This simple acknowledgment lets her know she was missed and emphasizes to everyone that each person's presence truly matters. We emphasize the importance of being together as a community by fostering an environment where attendance is valued and celebrated. It's vital for children to feel cherished and valued, so openly communicating our recognition of their absence fosters a positive atmosphere for all!

Teachers, how do you address absentees in your classrooms? Do you let your students know they were missed when they return to school after an absence? If you haven't been doing this, consider starting to connect with them this way. If they do not hear those words, it may seem to them that no one noticed they were not at school. Children of all ages benefit from knowing they were missed when absent. Do you ask your students why they were absent? This is important information to gather, as many underlying issues can lead to children being absent from school.

Teachers, you are essential to shaping a child's educational journey! Your daily attendance is just as important as our children's. Our children learn a lot from our behavior. I've seen instances where, without prior notice to the leadership team, groups of eight to ten teachers called in sick for several days, sometimes followed by others doing the same. This created challenges, as there weren't enough substitutes to cover those classes, and students were often relocated to the gym during those times. It's a trend I've noticed among teachers in different districts, where calling out can feel like a way to express concerns to the administration. We must work together to find solutions that prioritize effective communication and ensure our students continue to thrive! Your commitment truly makes a difference!

Children possess a remarkable intuition for the atmosphere in their school environment! They quickly pick up on when everything is running smoothly and when it's not. Educators must set aside their differences and prioritize a child's learning, especially when it comes to matters they can't control. Let's create a nurturing atmosphere where our students can thrive!

Coaches, have you ever considered adding a few extra students to your team as mentors? Imagine the difference we can make for those who could thrive with a bit of support! While it's easy to focus solely on skill sets, let's not forget the extraordinary individuals seeking guidance, a sense of belonging, or a way to escape challenging situations. We nurture character and accountability by embracing these opportunities and creating a stronger, more united team. Victory isn't just about winning games, but also about uplifting everyone involved. Together, let's embrace this vision and make a lasting impact!

Let's prioritize increasing student participation on each team to transform our school culture! Engaging more students fosters sportsmanship, accountability, and vital character growth. Together, we can nurture these individuals into incredible team members, making it a worthwhile investment in our shared future! Let's embark on an exciting journey to transform our school culture! Every child is a treasure, and by investing just 30 to 60 minutes each week, we can uplift all students, no matter their skills. Together, we'll create an environment where our students and school thrive! Let's make a meaningful impact!

Let's inspire our older students to step into the rewarding role of peer mentors! This fantastic opportunity fosters openness and supports the growth of everyone involved. By hosting a weekly clinic, mentors can share their skills and knowledge, creating a vibrant learning environment. This approach strengthens our team's bonds and enhances our collective performance. Together, we can thrive and achieve great things!

Tracking student attendance and behavior daily is vital for their growth and success! This approach helps identify areas for improvement and promotes accountability in our school community. It's all about creating a positive and inclusive culture where every student feels valued and respected. Coaches across all school districts should embrace this practice wholeheartedly. We've noticed some students fall through the cracks due to insufficient support. Still, with transparent communication, we can ensure that every child shines in extracurricular activities without fear of rejection. We can make this vision a reality through thoughtful strategies and collaboration! Let's champion our students and help them thrive!

We believe in celebrating our children's unique qualities rather than fixating on their challenges. Appreciating them just as they are at every stage of their journey is essential. They'll surely shine with the right coach or mentor by their side! It might take some time, but they will reach their full potential with patience and support. Always hold onto hope, and wonderful things will happen!

Dear coaches and mentors, your dedication is truly inspiring! Imagine the fantastic possibilities if we all stretch our creativity a bit more. Let's also contact our school team members to recruit volunteers and tap into community partners for additional resources to expand our students' potential.

Extracurricular activities serve as an excellent tool for accountability. They encourage participants to reflect on their current situations while uncovering opportunities for improvement. They inspire us to ask important questions: Are we making the best daily decisions for our children's well-being? Are we truly seeing the positive growth outcomes we hope to achieve together? Count Me Present champions transparency and accountability for athletes and scholars every day, ensuring their voices are heard and their contributions are recognized.

Chapter 3

Learned Behavior

I want to begin by stating that I have interacted with thousands of parents. Each interaction is significant when we possess knowledge about the behavior we wish to change. Each family was unique, and I treated them with respect. I was assertive about the necessary changes needed for the benefit of our children. It is interesting to see how learned behavior can impact various aspects of our lives, including our behavior within schools and families. Addressing these learned behaviors is essential for fostering a positive and accountable learning environment for students. I kept an open dialogue with families to encourage participation and make adjustments to the agreements and interactions established for their children's overall growth. To truly respect families, we must be open and willing to listen, so that we can capture and understand the specific underlying issues affecting each family. We must avoid judgment and strive to understand others' perspectives before criticizing or gossiping about the issues affecting their children's accountability.

Accountability at school is crucial for maintaining a positive learning environment and ensuring that all students have the opportunity to succeed. It includes holding students, teachers, and administrators accountable for their actions and performance throughout every school year. When a culture of accountability exists in a school, it can result in higher academic achievement, improved behavior, and a stronger sense of fairness and integrity. All members of the school community must recognize and fulfill their responsibilities to create a productive and supportive educational environment. The experience of meeting with our parents and students has taught me the value of empathy and compassion. The behaviors observed in school districts or schools are often learned behaviors.

How is the behavior, which I have observed in our families, displayed as learned behavior? One reason is that many of our parents and guardians have adopted a system that works for them, allowing them to avoid complying with the standards set by our schools. These behaviors will be passed down through generations as part of their value system. Families may develop specific coping mechanisms to avoid complying with school standards. To better understand a particular family's behavior, it is essential to identify students' absenteeism patterns. On which day of the week do the children in this family tend to be absent from school most often? There may be a specific day of the week when absenteeism is more common within a particular family.

What do the letters from the parents or guardians to the school say regarding each absence? How many children in the family are of school age? Are all school-age children enrolled in a school? I have discovered that one student may not be enrolled for some unknown reason. Is the attendance of all students in that family consistent across other schools? Who is responsible for writing the absentee letter regarding the student's absences? Is it the parents or the students? Attendance personnel should not be taking handwritten absentee notes from our children. There are too many high school students writing notes about their absences from school. Every note surrounding our children's attendance should be written and signed by the parent or guardian. Tracking notes regarding a student's attendance will provide clearer outcomes and highlight behaviors that affect our attendance standards. How can we break the cycle surrounding the behavior we want to change? We introduce parents and guardians to an intervention that will help them change their behavior.

Let's take a closer look at the impact of learned behaviors within our schools. These behaviors play a crucial role in the problem of truancy, where absenteeism becomes a troubling norm. Numerous families face a range of challenges—financial struggles, personal issues, and a lack of support—that can drive their children to miss school. A barrage of excuses often masks this cycle of absenteeism. It is time we recognize that these aren't just excuses; they are signals of deeper issues that need to be addressed to foster a more supportive educational school environment.

I had the opportunity to meet with the Jacob family and discuss the importance of implementing an assessment for their child. During our conversation, the mother expressed her concerns, saying, "I keep him home because he shakes a lot, Mrs. Winfield, like he is having seizures." At that moment, the child began shaking profusely. I remained calm and attentive. The mother continued, explaining that there are times when "he kicks, and I find it hard to calm him down or get him to respond." As she spoke, the student began to imitate the behavior. In response, I said, "Stop, stop, stop!" Immediately, the student ceased exhibiting the behavior the mother had suggested was the reason for his many absences from school. The mother gazed at me, realizing that the behavior she had shared would no longer be acceptable, given the reason the student was absent from school. The student became an outstanding student. The mother agreed with the intervention, and no modifications were ever needed for this student. The mother complied with the standards put in place for the student's betterment. The student showed significant growth in school due to his improved daily attendance. Every intervention should demonstrate accountability on behalf of the family. If the intervention does not reflect accountability on behalf of the family, you will not see any results. Accountability within our schools yields better results and outcomes.

In the southern region of the country, school typically starts in the first or second week of August; however, some families choose to register their children after Labor Day, which I had the opportunity to observe throughout the years. Another group would register their children but wait until after

Labor Day to send them to school. This is a cultural phenomenon that affects some school districts throughout our country. How do we combat this behavior? How can we shift the mindset regarding families registering their children and ensuring they are accounted for in our schools before Labor Day? This has been a challenge, and we still face the same concerns related to our children starting school on the first day of the school year. Many people say, "It is because of uniforms," that the children are registered late or do not come to school until after Labor Day. While many school districts have invested in student uniforms and supplies, this initiative has not led to any positive changes in student behavior. We started working with families to ensure their children were registered and attending school before Labor Day. Some school districts started early registration before the end of the prior school year, thinking this would help. Unfortunately, this learned behavior has affected many school districts throughout the southern United States.

I had the opportunity to meet the Abraham family during a school year after Labor Day. The Abraham family was unique. The principal informed me that all the students in this particular family had missed over 40 days of school in the previous year. She wanted me to work with the mother to identify the reasons behind the children's excessive absenteeism. The principal asked me to develop strategies to encourage regular student attendance. I thought something was wrong. It had to be an underlying issue to keep the children from attending school. I quickly realized that no underlying issues were preventing the children from attending school. The school never met with the family to discuss the behavior, and therefore, the family felt there was no reason to change it. All the students within the Abraham family were in elementary school. It was a behavior that the family had learned and implemented for their convenience. The Abraham family received an intervention plan that was implemented for the entire school year. The intervention plan was effective, and no modifications were made to it. The mother adhered to the plan without any pushback. The Abraham children began attending school regularly. This allowed teachers to assess them more closely and found that they were all gifted. Is this information important? Of course it is. This enables teachers to provide additional resources for children and develop a more engaging curriculum, thereby fostering their growth. We would never have discovered this information if they had continued to be absent from school. The children went from being frequently absent to having perfect attendance. They excelled academically, and the parents were thrilled to see their children's progress.

A new opportunity arose for me to work with the Isaac family for an entire school year, which presented a significant challenge. The mother had a limited income and could wash clothes only once a month. The child experienced bedwetting, and whenever this happened, the mother would keep her home from school until she had enough money at the beginning of the month to do the laundry. The mother did not share this information with the school because she felt embarrassed. After identifying the issue preventing the child from attending school, I discussed it with the school's leadership team. The leadership team granted the mother access to the school's washer and dryer, allowing her to keep her child's clothes clean and ensuring the child was accountable during school hours. There are thousands of stories that are hindering our children from attending school daily. Out of the thousands of stories, not one made me feel the child had the right not to be accountable during school hours.

How can we break the cycle of behaviors we want to change? We can introduce parents and guardians to an intervention that will empower them to help modify these behaviors. Our approach must emphasize accountability from both the family and the school. For instance, we cannot hold elementary children accountable for their attendance issues; instead, our primary focus should be on their parents and guardians. Elementary school students need someone to intervene and implement strategies that will support their growth.

I started meeting with parents and guardians to inform them about the laws related to their children's daily attendance. During our initial meeting, I emphasized the need for behavioral changes regarding attendance. I also gave parents and students the opportunity to share any underlying issues that may be affecting the child's school attendance. If the information shared by the parents or guardians was not life-threatening, then a contract and intervention were put in place. If the issue affecting the family required resources beyond my control, I directed the Guidance Counselor or Administration to meet with the student or parent. I held weekly meetings with school personnel to update them on any changes regarding the students' daily attendance.

Often, I would receive calls in the morning from parents reporting that their child had a stomachache or headache. I would advise them, "Give them an aspirin or Tylenol and send them to school." Not every minor ailment warrants a child's absence from school. Most schools have a nurse available to assist with any unforeseen health issues that may arise in our students. If a child is not sick enough to see a doctor, are they ill?

I met a mother who had several children, and she would often openly talk about the outings she had planned for the next day. Unbeknownst to her, her children were secretly making plans to join her. The next morning, all of them claimed they weren't feeling well. After meeting with the mother several times, we discovered that the children were pretending to be ill so they could accompany her on the outings. Once the mother changed the way she communicated about various outings, we began to see a significant improvement in the children's daily attendance.

Many behaviors in children are learned, which means we need to be strategic in our efforts to change them. Some parents may resort to manipulation to achieve their desires. It's important to remember that we are dealing with these learned behaviors. Families often operate under their own set of rules, and they may view the standards set by schools as a threat to their established behavior.

I find it surprising that many students are promoted to the next grade despite missing an excessive number of school days, with little to no action taken regarding their attendance. How can children be promoted when they have missed an entire school semester? Remember, the Abraham children had missed over 40 days of school before I implemented an intervention. I have observed this issue happening too frequently in our school districts. This situation sends a troubling message to other parents that such behavior is acceptable.

We must improve accountability for both parents and children concerning attendance outcomes. Without some form of intervention to encourage change, these students' behaviors will not improve. Parents need to cooperate with schools to address the underlying issues that prevent their children from attending school regularly. Promoting students who have poor attendance does not benefit them.

We are preparing our children for life beyond the school years. If we do not teach them the importance of regular attendance and the standards that go with it, we are not helping them succeed. Truant students may experience a range of adverse outcomes, including academic setbacks, decreased school engagement, a higher likelihood of dropping out, and an increased risk of involvement in harmful behaviors. Addressing truancy early is crucial for helping students remain on track. Truant students present a significant challenge for both schools and communities. To effectively tackle truancy, it is essential to understand the underlying reasons for this behavior and to collaborate with families in finding solutions that encourage regular school attendance. Approaching this issue with empathy and a willingness to cooperate with families is vital for addressing the root causes of truancy. A call to action is to inform parents that if they need assistance with truancy or have specific questions about this issue, they are welcome to request more information.

A meeting should ideally have been called when the student reached three unexcused absences from school. If school administrators are hesitant to have difficult conversations with parents, they may want to consider pursuing a different profession. We need to address the issues that prevent our children from reaching their full potential. I always tell the leaders within schools, "We make things right by exposing what is wrong."

Accountability begins with establishing a dialogue between us and our parents and guardians about the behavior that needs to change. It is crucial to hold ourselves and others accountable for our actions and behavior. Accountability encourages us to take responsibility for our choices and their consequences, while also promoting trust and respect in relationships. When we are accountable, we demonstrate integrity and a willingness to learn from our mistakes.

Remember, the impact of attendance on student engagement and learning outcomes is a significant topic in educational research. Research has demonstrated a positive correlation between regular attendance and academic performance. Students who attend classes consistently are more likely to engage in the learning process, participate in discussions, and complete assignments on time. This active involvement often leads to a better understanding of the material and improved learning outcomes. Conversely, poor attendance can result in disengagement, missed learning opportunities, and ultimately, lower academic achievement.

Educators must consider attendance when designing interventions to support student success. It is crucial to address the issues affecting our school outcomes directly and effectively. Why should a teacher be held responsible for a student's poor test scores if the student has a history of poor attendance and was promoted without any intervention regarding this behavior?

The behavior of these students will not change unless their parents are willing to collaborate with the school to address the underlying issues that prevent their children from attending school regularly. Truancy is a significant issue that impacts many schools and families. It refers to a student's absence from school without a valid excuse or permission. Truancy can lead to serious consequences for a student's academic performance, social development, and future opportunities. Several factors contribute to truancy, including family circumstances, peer influence, disengagement from school, and underlying behavioral or emotional issues. It is essential to acknowledge that truancy often reflects broader issues in a student's life or the family environment.

Addressing truancy requires a comprehensive approach that involves collaboration among schools, parents, and community resources. Effective interventions may include early identification of at-risk students, offering support and resources to families, implementing positive reinforcement strategies, and creating a school environment that fosters engagement and a sense of belonging.

Add student transfers to the list of learned behaviors. Parents or guardians will transfer a truant student every school year during December or January. This practice allows families to feel that the days of truancy at one school are erased when they enter a new school's database system. All schools within the district must adhere to the same standards, as this promotes transparency and facilitates change. I have listened to thousands of stories explaining why a child was habitually absent from school. Yet, I never encountered a story that convinced me the child was justified in being unaccountable during school hours.

Ultimately, addressing truancy requires empathy, understanding, and a commitment to finding sustainable solutions that support the well-being and success of all students. One effective way to combat truancy is to establish strong partnerships and communication between schools, parents, and community organizations. By working together, these stakeholders can identify the root causes of truancy and develop targeted interventions to address them. Additionally, implementing early intervention programs, such as mentoring or counseling, can support students at risk of chronic absenteeism. Schools can also utilize data tracking and analysis to identify patterns of truancy and implement personalized strategies to support individual students.

Furthermore, creating a positive and engaging learning environment can help to motivate students to attend school regularly. These are just a few practical ways to combat truancy and promote regular school attendance. We can no longer accept learned behaviors in our schools that do not promote positive outcomes. We must establish standards for our children and parents to follow in our school environment. It should be our first mission to identify the learned behavior from our students and parents. Secondly, we need to be transparent about our standards by holding both students and parents accountable for not adhering to the guidelines we have established in our school environment. These standards are crucial for the growth of our children. "Learned Behavior" refers to actions that need to be adjusted by the standards we set.

Chapter 4

Attendance Laws/Attendance Classes

School districts should review their attendance data daily to identify areas for improvement and address any issues promptly. Since absentee reports are updated daily, it's essential to stay informed. Has your district ever considered offering parent attendance classes? These classes are different from Student Attendance Review Board meetings and can be scheduled on Saturdays to accommodate work schedules. They aim to provide valuable information about the importance of a child's daily attendance. The classes will educate principals, attendance staff, teachers, students, and their parents or guardians about the attendance laws in their state. Participants will learn about the consequences of violating truancy laws, benefiting all stakeholders involved. By offering these classes, school administrators can help prevent truancy behavior and support students in overcoming obstacles to stay in school. These classes are designed to address various challenges that children face, including academic struggles, gang involvement, teen pregnancy, parental control issues, and poor decision-making. The district can decide when these classes will be offered to their parents and students. I suggest holding a one-hour class on Saturdays once a month for parents who are unable to attend during school hours. The school district has access to various tools and resources that can help parents support their child's daily attendance.

Below are several topics that can be covered in the district's mandatory classes.

1. Enforcing the State's Truancy Laws
2. Consequences for Violating Truancy Laws
3. Consequences of Poor Decision-Making

4. Gang Prevention
5. Teen Pregnancy
6. Future Opportunities for Graduates vs. Dropouts
7. Parental Involvement
8. Workforce Development

You can ask your District Attorney's office to give these classes to discuss the laws in your state regarding attendance. A mandatory one-hour class per month or semester for parents who require additional support can yield dividends for your school district. Keep in mind that you have numerous resources to help you improve your attendance standards. Truancy is a crime in most states. Your District Attorney is an elected official. Their office ensures that local laws are upheld and manages the consequences for those who fail to comply with the governing rules.

I worked with an excellent District Attorney's Office in my county. The District Attorney was highly engaged in initiatives to encourage our children to attend school. Her office implemented various incentives for students throughout the community, including giving away bikes to elementary- and middle-school students who maintained perfect attendance for the entire school year. I can confidently say her efforts have led to positive changes for our students. If your school district leaders are not meeting regularly with your county district attorney, they should start doing so. Building these relationships is essential if we want to achieve real change regarding our schools' attendance data. Accountability at all levels is critical. We need to discuss attendance laws to help our parents and students better understand the laws governing our community and state.

Truancy is punishable by law in most states. While we don't want to upset our parents, there are moments when we need to capture their attention. In doing so, it may be necessary to discuss the laws governing student attendance and absences. Being accountable means understanding these laws, which empower us to advocate for the standards required to ensure our children's growth and success.

Our county's Department of Human Services began collaborating with us by requesting that parents provide a copy of their child's attendance record for re-certification of state benefits. Our children must be accounted for during school hours, as many crimes in major cities occur then. If our children are not held accountable during school hours, there is a significant risk that they will engage in these criminal activities.

We need to prioritize our children's future by fostering self-sufficiency as they prepare to leave high school. Educating them about accountability can truly transform their lives. By instilling a sense of responsibility, we can help our children become self-sufficient and lead productive lives after high school.

I would occasionally receive a call from a community police officer during the school day, informing me that they had a student from one of our schools with them and asking for my advice on what they should do. I would tell the officer that taking them to Juvenile Court wouldn't benefit anyone, but that bringing them to school would benefit everyone. For any students found throughout the school day, I would instruct the officers to contact me so that I could return to the school to contact the parents and meet with the students to discuss the behavior. Allowing the officers to bring those students to the school enabled me to review their overall attendance record and grades.

I would have the student write a letter on "The Importance of Attending School." I would contact the parent or guardian to inform them that the student needed to be picked up from my office before they could be released. I would allow the student to return to class after writing the letter. I would instruct the student to report back to my office after school so that we could meet with the parent or guardian together. During the meeting, the student was allowed to read their letter to the parent about "The Importance of Attending School." We discussed the students' attendance and grades. I would then put a written intervention plan in place for the student, which both the parent and the student would sign. I viewed the intervention as a contract between the student, the parent, and me. I have never had the same student brought to the school by a community police officer more than once.

Another factor affecting the school's culture is teen pregnancy. Each year, we see several female students who get pregnant within various school districts. How does your district work with these students? Indeed, these students will likely have numerous doctor appointments and/or sick days surrounding their pregnancy. How do you address these concerns? I believe the sooner you can get these students homeschooled, the better it will be for your attendance and the school's overall culture. Remember, all students' attendance is counted for the overall attendance rate. We need to provide accommodations expeditiously for those students in our environment.

Another common problem is the end-of-semester celebrations. How can we solve this common problem? One recommendation is to eliminate celebration days before school breaks at the end of the semester. I have observed that many school districts hold end-of-semester parties or celebrations right before the break. This sends a discouraging message to both parents and students, as very few students return to school after these celebrations. This issue also extends to end-of-year celebrations. When should you have the celebrations? They should be held no sooner than the last day of the break. Every student needs to be in school and counted for each day. Celebrating too quickly inadvertently sends the wrong message to our parents and students. I once had a parent tell me that "the days leading up to a break or the end of the school year do not matter." However, it is essential to understand that every day counts. We should not give the false impression to our parents and students that the first day of school is more critical than the last day. According to the Department of Education, every day is equally important. Please remember the following: Keep the pizza parties, barbecues, and May Day events scheduled for the last day of classes. Daily attendance is crucial! Don't celebrate too early. Remember, if more than 5% of your student body is absent for a day or more, your attendance rate will significantly decline.

Holding end-of-semester exams until the last day before break is advantageous. Many students believe they can skip returning to school after the exam until the following week. Stop administering tests too early in the school year. It sends a negative message to both our students and their parents. Every day of school is essential; even a single day's absence can negatively affect attendance rates. Your state and school district evaluate your school's attendance performance, and this information is publicly available. Don't compromise your standards and educational outcomes by rushing into testing. Every school day holds the same significance as the first day of school. When a parent asked me what the most important day of school is, I responded that every school day is equally important. The last day of school is just as important as the first day of school. Every day, we should ensure that all our students are present in school. To celebrate the end of the school year, I would organize pizza parties for my students on the last day of school. Trust me, on the last day, every student was accounted for. I made a conscious effort to be attentive to those days that could have led to a decline in attendance. I'm not referring to the senior schedule; we all know it's different.

Recently, I visited a family in Jacksonville, North Carolina, on the last day of school for the students. I asked the student, "Are you happy that the school year is over? Did you attend school today?" The young lady responded, "Yes." Her mother added, "She had to attend school, Ms. Susie, because they had their end-of-the-year exam today." I was elated to see that some school districts are doing things right; every day of school is significant. Being accountable on the first day of school is just as crucial as on the last day.

I have researched many school district attendance standards. I have identified a few districts where I believe their attendance standards are unrealistic. One particular district's policy regarding student absences struck me as overly harsh. It was not only harsh on the student but also on the district as a whole. If a student has 10 or more unexcused absences, they must repeat that grade. Are you kidding? Again, we cannot harm the entire school district by setting unrealistic standards and goals for our children. This standard will not only set the student back, but also set the school district back, as it relates to its graduation cohort. The standard mentioned above is very aggressive. Nobody is considering the consequences as they relate to the graduation cohort. This standard will affect the graduation cohort for many years to come. Remember, the graduation rate depends on when a particular student is expected to graduate from high school. If the student does not graduate, it will be reflected in the school's graduation cohort report. We will discuss the graduation cohort in more detail in a later chapter. The Department of Education tracks these student groups. The graduation rate for those high schools depends on the number of students within their cohort who graduated during their appointed year. We must be knowledgeable about the standards we set for our children and parents to grow. Are the standards measurable? Are they realistic? Are they goal-oriented for the students? Will the standards we implement create a positive change within our school environment?

We should never forget. Do not establish a standard that causes more harm than good. "Count Me Present" sounds much better than "Count Me Absent."

Chapter 5

Interventions and Incentives

Suppose you have approximately 20 students or fewer who are frequently absent. How can you address their daily attendance behavior? I suggest that your school counselor or attendance staff implement a specific intervention for these students. Here are some recommended steps to establish a higher standard for younger students' attendance behaviors:

1. Have daily check-ins with those students.
2. Allow those students a chance to have their voices heard.
3. Inform parents about the intervention during the initial conference regarding the student's attendance.
4. Create some incentives for those students to work toward. Allow the student to share what incentive they would like to work toward. The incentive should not be valued at more than $10 and should not be in monetary form.
5. Start slowly by providing a weekly incentive for good attendance or behavior, and as the student progresses, transition to biweekly incentives, then monthly and semesterly incentives. Before long, the student will have assisted you in correcting their attendance and behavioral outcomes.

The interventions/incentives that are being put in place to change the behavior should not be candy or chips, etc., as too many of our children are struggling with health concerns due to their diet. The first incentive should be something as small as an attendance board with the student's name. Allow the student to visit your office daily to receive a star for each day they are present, which they can then display next to their name. If a modification is needed for the student within the first two weeks, you can implement a significantly larger incentive to encourage the student's growth. The incentives should be something personal, such as a toy truck, car, yo-yo, doll, or paint set. We need every student who is assigned to our schools to succeed. Suspensions will only hinder the school's data and create a barrier to the school's overall growth for the school year. Remember, we are implementing incentives to help us change the negative behavior. These incentives will not reward students who require additional support for negative behavior. Additional support will result from raising standards in our schools. We do not change our children; instead, we modify the standards that lead to the desired change in their behavior and in our families.

What about the remaining student population? How can we ensure their attendance continues to thrive? To keep our children motivated to attend school daily, we must also start to reward good behavior. For example, perfect attendance is a significant accomplishment for a student. Attending school for 180 days or longer without missing a day is an outstanding accomplishment for a student. How do we celebrate such an accomplishment? We must celebrate LOUDLY. It would be great to have an attendance board (marquee) in the school to show the other students the reward of being accounted for each day. This will raise awareness among students with perfect attendance, helping them stay motivated and focused on their goals. For those students who haven't missed any days, keep reminding them that they are setting a very high standard for their peers to follow. Keep it fresh in their minds that we see you! Applaud! Applaud! Applaud! Students love knowing they are doing something magnificent, and their peers can celebrate their accomplishment. The more you celebrate these achievements, the more you encourage other students to participate in and contribute to the celebration. If you do not celebrate these students loudly, their accomplishments will not benefit the student body or the school culture.

We should speak up about important issues, such as our students' attendance standards. By staying silent, we are not helping our students set goals for themselves. As a student, I appreciated receiving a ribbon each year for perfect attendance. This was an accomplishment that no one could take from me. I went to school, even on days that I didn't feel well. Why? What was the incentive that motivated me to attend? Simply put, I wanted that ribbon.

Let's look for creative ways to celebrate our children. For example, I would have a luncheon at the end of the school year to honor those students with perfect attendance. I would invite the parents to be a part of the celebration. I invited the parents because they were an integral part of the reason their child was present each day. I would have drawings for the students who were on the perfect attendance roster. There were fresh flowers on the tables, and the simple banquet menu consisted of deli sandwiches, chips, cookies, lemonade, and other light refreshments. The meal was not expensive, but the reason for the celebration was received with much love from both our parents and students alike. The celebration lasted about an hour to honor the students who made the sacrifice of attending each day.

I recall one mother, whose son had perfect attendance for the year, confiding in me that he had considered not coming to the event that day because his shoes had holes in them. The son won one of the gift cards during the drawing. The mother cried and said, "Mrs. Winfield, this gave me so much hope for my son to win one of the gift cards so that he can buy himself a pair of shoes." This also sent a message to the son about the importance of attending school each day.

Because celebrating our children's attendance achievements is so important, a small amount of funding should be allocated to support this effort. Administrators, please note that you do not need a large budget to implement incentives for your students. An investment of as little as $1,000 for your student population for the entire school year can be all that's needed. Those perfect attendance students each semester can get a T-shirt that says something like "Accountability Matters" or any slogan that represents your school. I would ensure it mentions their daily attendance. You can also purchase wristbands to give to students with perfect attendance each semester. The wristbands and T-shirts can serve as small incentives for the student population. There are also larger gift items that can be raffled off after each semester, such as a $30 tablet from an online retailer. You can also include several oversized items in the perfect attendance drawings during the honor roll ceremony. These students must be celebrated. They need to realize their efforts *are* being seen. I was thankful for the accomplishments that unfolded surrounding our students' attendance outcomes. Attendance rates were high, and I was elated to see our children not only being accounted for during school hours but also learning.

Some school district leaders need to change their mindset regarding funding. We should not be concerned about losing funding if the children within our district are accounted for each day and learning. In changing the school culture, school administrators must celebrate loudly at the school level. You can also get the district leaders to celebrate at the district level. I recommend doing both. All students need to see how rewarding perfect attendance is. I can promise you that if you celebrate loudly, the number of students with perfect attendance will increase each school year. The days of our district leaders sitting behind their desks should be over. Our School Board Members, District Leaders, and all stakeholders should also be attending these celebrations.

When do you inform students that incentives will be put in place for perfect attendance? It's on the very first day of school. I had the administration team at each elementary and middle school inform their students that they were competing against other schools within the district for attendance outcomes. Parents were bringing their students to school after morning appointments to ensure their child was accounted for during school hours. The attendance data soared. The high school students were competing individually to win a monetary gift card. The parents became involved, and the students were motivated throughout the school year. Your celebration doesn't have to look like mine, but it should involve some form of celebration.

Let's take a look at the other side of interventions. Implementing an intervention plan was a helpful tool that took place during a Student Attendance Review Board (SARB) meeting with parents and students to discuss the student's absenteeism. In this meeting, I would ask the student in front of their parents or guardians the following question. "What do you want to be when you grow up?" The student would state aloud their goal after finishing high school. Regardless of the student's grade level, I would instruct the student to name various professions they are inspired to pursue in life. The students would mention multiple professions such as teacher, doctor, nurse, counselor, mayor, firefighter, police officer, and military personnel. One middle school young lady said to me, "I want to do what you do, Mrs. Winfield." I would then instruct the student to look at their parent or guardian and share their aspirations for the future with them out loud. I wanted the parent to realize that the truant behavior was hindering the student's goals and aspirations. Many times, the parent would hear the child speaking and start crying because they did not understand the importance of the child attending school each day. It was during this time that the parent realized that truant behavior can destroy aspirations. I would send the student back to class and ask the mother or guardian how I could assist them in helping their child reach their full potential. Regardless of whether this was a lightbulb moment or a turning point for the family, it made the parents or guardians realize the vital role they play in helping their child attend school regularly. Engaging in these meaningful conversations allows us to be intentional about the interventions we implement on behalf of our children. Additionally, remember to document these discussions.

Next, let's discuss early dismissal. What percentage of students are checked out of school each day? Is it more than 3%, and what are the reasons for these early checkouts? If students are being dismissed for a doctor's appointment, does the school administration team request a doctor's note upon the student's return the following day? If not, why not? Recently, I was standing in a school building at about 1:15 p.m. when a mother asked for permission to check her student out. The receptionist asked the mother, "Why are you checking the student out of school early?" "No reason," the mother stated. This was the opportunity for the receptionist to inform one of the school administrators regarding this behavior. Our parents' behavior regarding our attendance standards will not change unless we express the behaviors we would like to see altered. Our parents will not understand how to improve if we remain silent.

We promote change by taking intentional steps to achieve the growth we want to see in our students and parents. "Interventions and Incentives" are just another way of being strategic. Interventions help us establish a plan of action, while incentives help students set goals and work toward them. These incentives can boost a student's confidence, particularly in terms of their daily attendance and academic performance. When used together, interventions and incentives are valuable resources that can transform attendance standards and the school's overall culture.

Chapter 6

Graduation Cohort

We eagerly awaited the moment we would walk across the stage to receive our high school diplomas. We didn't know at the time that the Department of Education was also waiting for us to graduate. Each state's Department of Education issues a comprehensive report card for every school, utilizing data collected from various metrics within each institution. These report cards typically assess key performance indicators such as student academic achievement, graduation rates, teacher qualifications, and overall school safety. By analyzing this data, stakeholders, including parents, educators, and policymakers, can gain valuable insights into the quality of education provided at each school and identify areas that may require improvement. Our task has become even more challenging due to the numerous transfers within and between districts. This situation also raises questions about learned behavior. We touched on the graduation cohort in an earlier chapter, so let's take a closer look at what is working concerning the graduation cohort. I am passionate about achieving a 100% graduation rate. How can we reach this goal? It is crucial that when a 9th-grade student enrolls in a high school for the first time, the school actively tracks that student's progress each year to ensure they are on track to graduate. We cannot wait until the year the student is scheduled to graduate to begin monitoring their performance. Finding a student who should be in the graduating cohort for a given year can be a daunting and exhausting task, particularly in large school districts with thousands of high school graduates each year. I experienced this firsthand when I was tasked with locating a specific student amidst a sea of graduates. The challenge often feels overwhelming due to the sheer volume of information and the urgency of the situation. However, I've come to realize that social media has significantly simplified this process for many school districts. Platforms like Facebook, Instagram, and LinkedIn enable educators and administrators to connect with students in ways previously unimaginable, enabling faster, more efficient communication. Utilizing these modern tools can make the difference between a frustrating search and a successful outreach.

Achieving a 100% graduation cohort is a significant goal that requires a strategic approach. First and foremost, the school's Administration Team should designate a dedicated individual to oversee this critical initiative. Maintaining a consistent focus on this task throughout the academic year is essential. When a student transfers after entering our school in 9th grade, it is crucial to gather comprehensive information to facilitate tracking their future progress. One effective method is to review the school district's database to determine if the student remains within the district. If the student is no longer enrolled, it's advisable to contact the school clerk from which the student transferred.

Taking a proactive approach in maintaining connections with students who have departed is crucial for facilitating their ongoing educational journey. It is essential to engage with these individuals to provide support and resources that might assist them in their future endeavors. In our outreach efforts, we may encounter heartbreaking situations, such as discovering that a former student has passed away. While it is never easy to uncover news of such a loss, we must handle the situation with sensitivity and respect.

When we receive confirmation of a student's death, we must gather the necessary documentation to ensure that we accurately reflect this information in our records. Acceptable forms of documentation may include an obituary, a newspaper article, or credible information from an online memorial site. This documentation is critical, as we must provide comprehensive data regarding the graduation cohort when reporting to the state's Department of Education.

We must account for every student involved in this process. Any oversight could result in significant penalties that might jeopardize our institution's graduation rate. To prevent such consequences, we must exercise meticulous attention to detail while approaching this sensitive matter with empathy and respect. This approach not only honors the memory of those who have passed but also ensures that we meet all regulatory compliance requirements effectively. By doing so, we uphold our commitment to our community and maintain the integrity of our institution.

How can we achieve a 100% graduation rate? This goal requires a systematic approach that begins with meticulous attention to data as soon as students enter high school in the 9th grade. During a recent visit to a school district, I sifted through numerous boxes of documents in an effort to locate the missing records of students who were unaccounted for in their graduation cohort. This experience highlighted a critical gap in tracking student progress. I want to commend the schools that have achieved a 100% graduation rate; your dedicated efforts and strategies are truly commendable. It is essential to recognize that achieving a 100% graduation rate is within reach for all educational institutions. Still, it requires a proactive, detailed approach to monitor and support students throughout their academic journey. By focusing on grade transitions and implementing targeted interventions where necessary, we can ensure that every student has the opportunity to graduate on time.

A high retention rate plays a crucial role in shaping the success of a graduation cohort. When students remain engaged and involved in their studies, it not only boosts their individual academic performance but also fosters a supportive learning environment for their peers. To ensure that students continue to make progress toward graduation, it is essential to implement targeted interventions. Options such as summer school programs can provide valuable academic support, enabling students to reinforce their learning, address knowledge gaps, and stay engaged with the curriculum. By facilitating these interventions, educational institutions can help students maintain their momentum and ultimately enhance their chances of graduating on time.

It's important to consider that some students may be incarcerated in a detention center. If this is the case, you can contact the detention facility to inquire whether the student has completed any coursework while in detention. This information can be crucial in demonstrating that they possess enough credits to meet graduation requirements. The good news is that certified teachers are actively working in our detention centers, providing high-quality educational instruction to students daily. These educators deliver a comprehensive curriculum, and students receive grades based on the coursework they complete during their detention period.

It is crucial to remember our homebound students, who are unable to attend school due to medical conditions and are typically confined to their homes or hospital settings. These students receive care and supervision from medical professionals, with the intensity varying depending on their individual needs. To support these students effectively, we must closely monitor their progress and well-being. This includes regular check-ins and assessments to gain a more comprehensive understanding of their educational needs. Additionally, establishing targeted interventions is vital to fostering meaningful communication between the home and school environments. This may involve creating tailored learning plans that account for their medical restrictions while ensuring they remain engaged with their curriculum. Utilizing technology for virtual learning, facilitating communication with teachers, and providing resources for parents can enhance their educational experience. Ultimately, fostering a strong support system will help our homebound students feel connected to their school community and promote their academic success.

Through my observations, I have noted that a significant number of students encounter considerable challenges when attempting to reintegrate into the school environment after an extended absence. These challenges often stem from several factors, including heightened social anxiety, gaps in their academic knowledge, and the disruption of their established daily routines. Such obstacles can severely impact their ability to adjust and succeed in a classroom setting. To effectively support these students during their transition, we should implement a range of tailored strategies. This could involve regular check-ins with counselors or mentors to provide emotional support and address any concerns they may have. Additionally, offering online learning resources can help bridge knowledge gaps and allow students to catch up at their own pace.

Creating gradual reintegration plans that outline a step-by-step approach for re-entering the school environment can also be beneficial. This may include phased participation in classes, starting with smaller groups or specific subjects, before gradually increasing their involvement in the whole curriculum. By ensuring that each student receives the necessary support, academically, emotionally, and socially, we can help them thrive upon their return. It is crucial to recognize that these students are just as valuable to our graduation cohort as any other students, and they deserve the same level of attention and support to succeed.

Recognizing and counting every student, regardless of their circumstances, is essential. Accurate data collection is another way to support and enhance your graduation cohort efforts. This approach ensures that no student is overlooked and that every opportunity for academic achievement is acknowledged. Let's start by creating a strategic plan for the graduation cohort at every high school. Tracking every high school student throughout each school year to make sure they are accounted for and on track to graduate.

Chapter 7

Power of Mentoring

We need to acknowledge that we are not only mentoring our students, but also their parents and guardians. Every relationship involves some degree of mentorship. In our daily interactions with friends and family, they not only provide support but also hold us accountable for our actions. Recently, I had the opportunity to read "The Speed of Trust" by Stephen M. R. Covey. As the author points out, the key factor that transforms everything is trust. While the book focuses on business leadership practices, it emphasizes the significance of trust in all types of relationships. This book has provided me with the opportunity to delve deeper into the expansive realm of mentoring.

According to Mr. Covey, trust is defined as "Trust means confidence." When we place our trust in someone, we inherently expect them to meet our expectations and fulfill our requests. This expectation is rooted in our confidence in their abilities and integrity. It is essential for us to maintain this confidence and to believe that the outcomes we anticipate will yield positive results in the future. The true power of mentoring begins with a commitment to self-reflection, demanding that we be open and honest with ourselves. It's crucial to stay true to the principles and decisions we establish, as these create the foundation for the growth and development of those we mentor. By cultivating an environment of trust and transparency, we can empower others to reach their full potential while also enhancing our own mentoring skills. Mentoring offers a valuable opportunity to engage in thoughtful, challenging discussions. One pertinent question that arises is whether our expectations for our parents might be set too high. However, we must consider that, as long as our expectations are consistent with the school district's standards, we are justified in holding them. This alignment ensures that we maintain a fair and realistic approach, recognizing the shared responsibility between educators and families in fostering a supportive learning environment.

During your intervention meetings with students and their parents or guardians, consider asking the following questions to facilitate productive discussions and gather valuable insights:

1. What specific goals do you hope to achieve through this intervention, and how do you envision these goals will positively impact the student?
2. Can you outline the steps you plan to take to implement the action plan effectively? What strategies do you believe will be most beneficial?
3. What specific types of support, resources, or involvement do you need from the students or parents to ensure the success of the intervention?
4. Who will take responsibility for monitoring the progress and outcomes of the intervention? What methods will be used to track these results?
5. What is the anticipated timeline for us to observe any changes or improvements in the student's situation as a result of this intervention?
6. Can you trust that the purpose of this intervention is genuinely focused on enhancing the well-being and academic success of the student?
7. How will we collaboratively define and measure success for your child throughout this process? What benchmarks will be established?
8. Is the proposed action plan feasible and realistic for your family's current circumstances? If you believe it is not, could you share the challenges or barriers you foresee?

The above questions encourage open dialogue and foster collaboration among all parties involved, ultimately creating a supportive environment for the student's growth and development. It's critical to acknowledge that our behavior significantly impacts both our actions and our words. The way we approach a situation can elicit either a positive or a negative response. Therefore, always begin by reassuring parents or guardians that the goal of daily school attendance is to foster their child's personal development and academic success.

In intervention meetings, it is crucial to refrain from discussing the necessity of these interventions in terms of improving attendance metrics. Instead, focus on the child's unique needs. Rather than fixating on data, trust that it will naturally enhance once students and their families actively engage with the proposed interventions. Parents and guardians can often discern when we genuinely care about their child's holistic well-being and educational experience. Throughout these meetings, avoid bringing up any references to improving school-wide attendance statistics. Concentrate instead on the individual student and their progress. Our success hinges upon keeping the student at the center of our conversations with parents and guardians. Mentors and leaders should prioritize maintaining clear and open lines of communication about the interventions in place and the student's journey toward achieving their personal and academic goals.

Moreover, we must adopt a culture of accountability by taking responsibility for our actions and outcomes, without blaming others when challenges arise. It is essential to regularly review interventions and adjust them as needed to meet the student's changing needs effectively. By doing so, we foster a supportive environment that encourages growth and improvement for all involved. Consistently demonstrate genuine care for others by showing it through your actions. This involves paying attention, being present in conversations, and actively listening to what others have to say. Respect the dignity of every individual, regardless of their role or status, by treating everyone with kindness and consideration. It's essential to follow through on your commitments, as this builds a foundation of trust and reliability. Simple acts of kindness—such as offering a supportive word, lending a helping hand, or simply smiling—can create a significant impact on someone's day. Therefore, ensure your expressions of care are genuine, not merely obligatory gestures. Avoid hurrying through your interactions; instead, take the time to engage sincerely with others. Show authentic concern for their well-being and feelings. Remember, the relationships we build on trust and mutual respect can be fragile and easily undermined by neglect or misunderstanding. Nurturing these connections requires continuous effort and attentiveness.

As a mentor or leader, it is crucial to ensure that you communicate accurate information and uphold transparency regarding student attendance within the school. This standard is vital for maintaining fairness and trust in the educational environment. I have observed situations in which a parent has developed a closer relationship with a school staff member. Consequently, this connection can lead to discrepancies in how the student's attendance is monitored and assessed. In these instances, the student's attendance may not be held to the same rigorous standards as their peers', creating an unequal playing field. All students must adhere to standardized attendance policies to maintain a fair and equitable educational environment for everyone involved. Establishing these consistent standards not only reinforces the integrity of the school's policies but also promotes a sense of responsibility among students and their parents.

Attendance issues may occur for any student, including those of some teachers, highlighting the importance of impartiality in addressing such situations. It is essential that, if a teacher's child fails to meet the district's attendance requirements, they be subject to the same documentation and consequences as their peers. This approach ensures transparency and accountability, emphasizing that all students are treated equally, regardless of their parents' positions within the school system. By maintaining these standards, we foster a culture of fairness and mutual respect within the educational community.

Mr. Covey shares that there are four cores of credibility:

1. Integrity
2. Intent
3. Capabilities
4. Results

Let us delve into the vital concept of integrity. At its core, integrity embodies honesty and moral principles. Our demonstration of integrity is intricately woven into our beliefs and values, serving as a guiding force in our interactions and decisions. As mentors, our integrity is most evident in how we communicate, what we wear, and how we engage with others. These elements collectively signal to those around us, especially children and parents, that we are trustworthy and reliable. It is this unwavering commitment to integrity that empowers us to create a significant impact in their lives, fostering the positive changes they need to flourish.

Moreover, establishing trust is crucial in cultivating healthy relationships with students and their families. Trust typically starts to build within the first minute of meeting someone, making those initial interactions especially important. Additionally, the information shared by our parents and students during these initial meetings carries significant weight and must be handled with the utmost care. Confidentiality is paramount; sensitive information should be disclosed only to team members who require it to contribute to interventions designed to support the family effectively. This ensures that our approach is both respectful of privacy and designed to provide meaningful assistance.

During the initial meeting, it is crucial to clearly communicate to parents or guardians that you will be sharing information about their child with specific staff members involved in their support. A thoughtful approach would be to ask, "Is it acceptable for me to share your child's intervention plan with the staff members who will be assisting?" It is essential to acknowledge that parents and guardians are frequently concerned about the privacy of their child's personal information, and they expect it to be handled with care and discretion in our schools. Building trust from the outset is essential for a productive partnership. By being transparent and forthright about how information will be shared, we can foster an environment of openness that encourages collaboration. This not only reassures parents about their child's welfare but also lays a solid foundation for addressing the behavioral changes we aim to support. Establishing this trust and clear communication early on paves the way for a more effective and supportive intervention process.

Author Edmund Chan, in "Mentoring Paradigms," shares that there are three core competencies of a mentor. The three competencies that the author mentions are:

1. The Mentor Who Shepherds
2. Teaching
3. Leading

Let's delve into the three concepts, focusing on student mentoring within the school environment. In a school setting, each of us embodies the role of a shepherd, guiding and leading our students and colleagues in various ways. The effectiveness of this guidance hinges on our leadership skills and the standards we establish. Being intentional is crucial when implementing any intervention designed to foster growth for our students and their families. Every action we take should align with our educational goals and thoughtfully consider the needs of those we serve. Effective mentoring should not only foster positive change but also directly impact the outcomes we aspire to achieve, ensuring that students thrive both academically and personally.

To facilitate ongoing development, maintaining open lines of communication after the initial intervention is critical. This can be achieved through regular check-ins and follow-up meetings. During the first meeting with a parent to discuss the intervention plan, it's essential to clearly articulate any changes to communication protocols. For example, please inform the parent that handwritten notes from home will no longer be accepted, as this change is made to streamline communication and ensure that all information is consistently documented and easily accessible. Providing clear guidelines helps foster a collaborative environment between educators and families, ultimately benefiting the student's educational journey. The text emphasizes the importance of recognizing and altering specific behaviors related to student attendance. A mentoring role, known as the "shepherding mentor," is crucial to this process. This mentor must possess a comprehensive understanding of the overall dynamics within their group, often referred to as the "flock." This understanding includes identifying the factors contributing to poor attendance and devising effective strategies to address and improve these conditions.

When examining our students' attendance data, we must carefully evaluate what it reveals. Does the data reflect healthy attendance patterns, indicative of active engagement and commitment, or does it point to troubling behaviors that signal disconnection or disengagement? It's essential to approach attendance not as a subjective notion of fairness but rather as a straightforward metric that categorizes attendance as either satisfactory or unsatisfactory. A student is either adhering to attendance expectations or failing to do so.

Throughout my experience, I have frequently encountered the notion that a student is "on the bubble." This phrase suggests that the student is precariously close to failing to meet attendance criteria. If this situation arises, it necessitates immediate and targeted intervention to support that student in moving away from this precarious position. I maintain a firm belief in distinguishing between right and wrong in terms of behavior, rejecting the notion of gray areas or subjective interpretations. It is imperative to rigorously assess whether the established standards for student attendance and engagement are being achieved. The data we collect will serve as a vital tool in this evaluation, providing concrete evidence to help us determine whether a student meets our expectations. It also enables us to make informed decisions for interventions as necessary.

As the shepherding mentor, it is crucial to assess whether your school district is providing sufficient training for attendance staff throughout the academic year. Practical training ensures that every staff member is well-equipped to understand and respond to the complex and changing behaviors that influence student attendance. To foster a supportive learning environment, all attendance personnel must have access to an up-to-date platform that allows them to track and analyze attendance patterns and behaviors that negatively impact overall school attendance rates. This platform should offer resources such as data analytics tools, behavior intervention strategies, and best practice guidelines. Moreover, experienced attendance personnel play a vital role in mentoring and supporting newcomers in the field. This mentorship could include regular training sessions, collaborative workshops, and opportunities for shadowing experienced staff during attendance interventions. By fostering a culture of collaboration and continuous professional development, we can refine our attendance strategies and ultimately enhance student outcomes. I trained a significant number of attendance personnel and served as their mentor, providing them with the necessary information they had previously lacked due to inadequate training. I allowed the attendance personnel to shadow me for a few days, enabling them to ask questions and observe how to track students' daily attendance at various levels. Mentoring is instrumental in driving positive change by offering personalized guidance and encouragement to students facing challenges. As a mentor or attendance staff member in a school environment, your primary responsibility is to monitor and record daily attendance diligently. This involves not only tracking absences but also understanding the context behind them, whether they stem from personal, academic, or social factors. By maintaining thorough records and fostering open communication with students and their families, we can collaboratively develop strategies to enhance student participation and overall well-being. Each proactive step in this process contributes to creating a supportive learning atmosphere where every student has the opportunity to thrive.

Let's explore the second competency, which focuses on teaching. Effective teaching requires us to be both strategic and intentional about the information we present to families regarding their children's education. We must possess a thorough understanding of the various interventions we implement to support our families successfully. Merely inviting families to the school and stating, "You need to send your child to school every day," is unlikely to result in compliance. Instead, we should deliver information about our state's attendance laws in a way that resonates with parents and guardians. This should not be a simple handout; instead, it should be thoughtfully integrated into the initial intervention plan. By doing so, we can guide families through these regulations and help them understand their importance in the context of their child's education.

Many parents may not be aware of the rules governing their children's attendance or the potential repercussions that may arise from non-compliance. Therefore, it's crucial to approach parents with empathy and clarity, providing them with resources and strategies that encourage positive attendance behaviors. By fostering an open dialogue and sharing actionable insights, we can collaborate with families to enhance attendance outcomes and ensure that every child has the opportunity to succeed in school. Effective educators can ask well-crafted, insightful questions that elicit genuine responses from parents and guardians most of the time. School staff rely on accurate and honest information to provide the best possible support for their students' academic and emotional needs. Transparency and open lines of communication are essential when sharing information with families. Building trust and establishing a strong rapport with parents is critical. This can be achieved by providing clear, precise details about a student's behavior, learning challenges, and individual needs. By doing so, school staff can tailor their interventions and support strategies to address each student's unique circumstances.

During initial meetings, it is crucial to pose challenging questions that may not have straightforward answers. Educators should approach these conversations with sensitivity and patience, allowing parents or guardians the necessary time to respond thoughtfully and effectively. This collaborative dialogue not only enhances understanding but also fosters a supportive partnership between families and school staff, ultimately benefiting the students' educational experience. Get personal with your parents and guardians. Let parents and guardians know that for their child to succeed, we need to ensure that the intervention being implemented is effective. The only way it will work is if the information being shared is factual.

Effective teaching and instruction involve a combination of strategies and techniques designed to foster understanding. To ensure that others grasp what you are trying to teach, establishing a foundation of trust is crucial. This trust catalyzes open dialogue and practical learning. It is vital to communicate to parents and guardians that their voices carry significant power and influence, and that their active involvement is essential to their child's academic and personal success. Engaging parents in this process not only boosts their confidence but also fosters a collaborative environment that benefits the entire school community. To create this supportive atmosphere, we must prioritize listening to parents without judgment. By genuinely valuing their perspectives and experiences, we can empower them to make meaningful contributions to their child's education and foster a stronger partnership between home and school. Ultimately, this collaboration yields positive outcomes for students, thereby enhancing their chances of success.

We are all leaders. When working in a school environment with children of any age group, we are providing some form of leadership. Every employee in a school environment plays a critical role and, consciously or unconsciously, exhibits some form of leadership throughout the day. We must be mindful of the behaviors we display in front of our students, as these actions can significantly impact their development and perception of leadership. We need to exercise caution when engaging in conversations, especially those that can be heard by our children. Just as adults can be drawn into gossip, so too can children, and they are keen observers of the interactions around them. As leaders within our schools, our behaviors are scrutinized by our students, who often analyze and discuss the character traits and ethical standards of the staff they encounter.

If we aspire to be true leaders, we must understand that our actions speak volumes. Modeling integrity, respect, and professionalism is imperative, as our students look to us for guidance and inspiration. By leading by example, we not only cultivate a positive, respectful school culture but also empower our students to adopt similar values as they grow. For example, during one school year, a student approached me with information regarding an inappropriate relationship between a male and female staff member. The student disclosed specific details about where these individuals were meeting within the school premises to engage in intimate interactions. Following this revelation, we launched a thorough investigation and, to our dismay, found that the student's observations were, unfortunately, accurate.

Such situations are profoundly concerning, as our students should never be exposed to or made aware of staff members' personal lives in such compromising or inappropriate ways. Leaders in an educational setting must consistently maintain the highest standards of professionalism, ethics, and integrity. Engaging in conduct that blurs the lines between personal and professional lives not only undermines the authority and respect that staff members command but also sets a troubling example for students, who depend on us for guidance and appropriate behavioral norms. Effective leadership requires a steadfast commitment to discipline that encompasses all aspects of behavior and decision-making. This commitment should not be selective or limited to actions that are merely convenient or immediately impactful; instead, it should encompass every interaction and decision in the school environment. Fostering a healthy, respectful, and safe atmosphere is crucial—not solely for the immediate well-being of our students but also for the overarching integrity and reputation of the school community as a whole. It is our responsibility to create an environment where students can learn and grow, free from the complications that arise from unprofessional conduct. We have spent some time looking at the three competencies. Do you think there is a competency that should have been mentioned but was missing? If so, build on your own competencies. Add to this list and make any necessary modifications.

Chapter 8

Generational Apathy Towards High School Diploma

In the 21st century, we continue to face significant challenges as high school educators teach students who are often the first in their families to graduate high school. During recent conversations with these students, many expressed a profound sense of pride, believing they had successfully broken the cycle of limited educational attainment that their families faced.

However, one particular young lady shared a deeply personal struggle. She articulated that, despite her aspirations, she felt an acute lack of emotional support from her family throughout her academic journey. The idea of earning her high school diploma weighed heavily on her; she feared it might create a rift between her and her family. She worried that they would perceive her achievements as a stark reminder of their unfulfilled educational dreams, which could lead to feelings of alienation and resentment. This perspective was challenging for her, as she grappled with the complexities of her aspirations versus her loyalty to her family.

As I reflect on her experiences, I find it increasingly difficult to grasp the full extent of her emotional turmoil. It serves as a poignant reminder of the multifaceted nature of education and its profound impact on family dynamics. Graduating from high school should be a joyous and celebratory occasion for all students, marking a significant achievement in their lives. Unfortunately, there are times when students feel anxiety or fear of rejection instead of pride when they reach this pivotal milestone. I have had the privilege of witnessing numerous graduation ceremonies where parents are filled with a mix of emotions, especially when their children break what they consider a long-standing family curse regarding educational attainment. In those moments, I observed tears of joy streaming down the faces of proud parents, while others shed tears of profound pain as they reflected on their own struggles and sacrifices. One mother poignantly articulated her feelings, stating that as her daughter walked across the stage to receive her high school diploma, it felt as though she, too, was finally obtaining her own diploma, symbolizing their shared triumph over adversity. This moment encapsulated not just individual achievement but the breaking of generational barriers, transforming a traditional rite of passage into a powerful family celebration.

How did we arrive at this point in the 21st century? Much of our current reality stems from behaviors and mindsets inherited from previous generations. It is essential to acknowledge that many students face significant barriers, including socioeconomic challenges, cultural expectations, and limited access to resources, which hinder their educational journeys. As a society, we must actively strive to help our children overcome these hurdles and appreciate the transformative power of education. This requires us to foster genuine connections with these young individuals, ensuring they feel supported and understood. We need to consistently encourage them and make intentional efforts to reach out, reminding them of their potential to break the cycle of generational apathy towards high school education. By investing in their aspirations and providing a stable network of support, we can empower them to pursue their academic goals and ultimately reshape their futures. Many of these children articulate the immense challenges they face as they strive to be the first in their families to reach significant milestones, whether educational or personal. They often feel overwhelmed by the pressures of their circumstances, leading them to believe that quitting is a more attainable option, especially when they lack a support system to hold them accountable for their decisions. I've observed a poignant situation in which four generations of a single family live in the same government housing apartment complex, illustrating the cyclical nature of their struggles and highlighting the need for greater resources and mentorship in their community.

During my time as an Attendance Specialist, I had the opportunity to work with a group of remarkable high school students. Among them were several who encountered significant challenges with reading; some were even struggling to read at a first-grade level. This situation was not just an academic hurdle; it also affected their overall confidence and engagement in school. I devoted time to building relationships with these students, understanding their unique backgrounds and the obstacles they faced. Many of them were young men who felt a mix of frustration and determination about their reading skills. It was heartening to see their eagerness to learn, as they often approached me with the hopeful question, "Could you teach me how to read?" Their desire for assistance was a powerful reminder of the importance of support and encouragement in education. I struggled with trying to wrap my mind around high school students who could not read or write. I sent a letter to our superintendent at the time because it was overwhelming. I did not receive a response from the superintendent regarding the exact number of students who struggle with reading and writing. In my research, I discovered that school districts facing higher levels of need, particularly in literacy and attendance, tend to receive greater federal funding. This funding is often allocated to support targeted programs that aim to improve educational outcomes for these vulnerable student populations.

If you are reading this book, I implore you to take a decisive stand and become an outspoken advocate for our children, even if it means standing alone in the face of opposition. We have the power to bring about meaningful change by bravely exposing the injustices and shortcomings that exist within our educational system. Silence will not serve us; nothing will improve if we keep our concerns and insights to ourselves about the vital issues that impact our students' lives. Our children depend on you to be a voice that champions their needs and rights. Each of us has a significant role to play in shaping a brighter future for the next generation. The alarming truth is that far too many of our children are slipping through the cracks of a system that should be nurturing and protecting them. Let us not disregard the reality that our most valuable assets are our children—their potential, dreams, and well-being must always take priority. Together, we can work towards creating an environment where every child has the opportunity to succeed and thrive. The literacy crisis among young people aged 15 and older who cannot read or write represents a pandemic that is significantly more serious than COVID-19. This troubling situation has developed over many years due to various factors, including inadequate educational resources, socio-economic challenges, and systemic inequities. It is essential to recognize that we did not arrive at this point overnight, and addressing the complexities of this issue will require a sustained and concerted effort across communities, educational systems, and policy-making bodies. Solving this problem will take time, collaboration, and a commitment to ensuring every young person has access to quality education and the skills necessary for their future.

During my tenure in a different school district under state oversight due to unsatisfactory performance, I encountered a troubling situation at a particular school. Curious about the academic challenges the students faced, I approached the principal and asked, "Why are the children not performing at the same learning levels as their peers in neighboring districts?" The principal explained that the district had a troubling practice of reallocating teachers who had previously struggled at other schools throughout the region to this specific area of the city. This decision, driven by a misguided attempt to address staffing shortages, significantly hindered students' educational growth. As a result, many children were left without the strong academic foundation they needed, further deepening the inequities in their learning experience. The situation arose primarily due to constraints imposed by teachers' contracts, along with various factors affecting educators' working conditions and morale.

These issues persisted for over two decades, adversely affecting the quality of education provided. Ultimately, the state's intervention became necessary, leading to the assumption of control over these schools to rectify longstanding problems and enhance the educational environment for both teachers and students.

Parents need to understand the significant impact that student absences can have on learning. Each day a student misses school means missing crucial lessons and knowledge that may be difficult to acquire later, especially in a fast-paced curriculum where concepts build on one another. Consequently, both parents and students need to acknowledge the long-term effects of missed school days, not only on knowledge retention but also on skill development and overall academic performance.

Recently, I found myself engaged in a thought-provoking conversation with one of my students, who asked, "Mrs. Winfield, how many days do you think a student should attend school?" This inquiry not only prompted reflection but also underscored the critical importance of consistent attendance. Students need to remain committed to their education, as success in an academic environment requires active engagement and participation. In response, I explained that there are 180 instructional days in the school year, and it is vital for every student to be present each day. Regular attendance is crucial because each day builds on the last; missing even a single day can create gaps in knowledge and understanding that are difficult to bridge. We should never convey to our children that it is acceptable to miss several days, as this can set a concerning precedent regarding their educational responsibilities.

While we acknowledge that there are legitimate reasons for absences, such as illness or unexpected personal circumstances, it is essential to underscore the significance of daily attendance in our educational institutions. Consistent attendance plays a crucial role in enhancing academic performance and laying a solid foundation for learning. It is vital for all of us—students, teachers, and parents alike—to prioritize daily classroom presence.

Regular attendance enables students to engage fully with the diverse and enriching learning experiences provided each school day. Through active participation, students can grasp complex concepts, collaborate effectively with peers, and contribute to a vibrant classroom environment that fosters growth and critical thinking.

Moreover, we must confront the reality that if we do not transform the prevailing culture around attendance within our schools, we will continue to observe the same disappointing outcomes. We must work together to cultivate an atmosphere that values and encourages consistent attendance, ensuring that every student has the opportunity to reach their full potential.

Chapter 9

The Data Tells a Story

As we rigorously examine and review various data sets, it becomes evident that each data point reveals a unique story that can transform our understanding of broader trends. The responsibility for interpreting this data rests squarely with the reader, requiring a blend of analytical skills and context knowledge. To facilitate this analysis, I developed a comprehensive attendance model that effectively captures and analyzes daily attendance fluctuations. This model is not just a tool; it is a strategic asset that enabled me to track key performance objectives and outcomes, thereby enhancing our ability to monitor progress and make informed decisions.

By interpreting the data through this enhanced lens, I could align our strategies more precisely with our organizational objectives, resulting in meaningful improvements in student attendance and engagement. To ensure accurate progress tracking, I adopted a systematic approach that went beyond generating daily reports. Each day, I would meticulously compile and run the attendance report, then thoroughly review the previous day's findings. This routine enabled me to scrutinize fluctuations and variations in the data, thereby identifying patterns and trends that were crucial for informing strategic decisions.

This ongoing analysis became an essential component of my daily workflow, providing valuable insights that deepened my understanding of our student population and refined our approach to it. Through this rigorous process, I was able to pinpoint where attendance changes occurred and identify which specific students contributed to the shifts reflected in the data. This targeted tracking enabled examination of individual student attendance patterns, illustrating how students transition between different levels of compliance and non-compliance in their daily attendance.

My attendance tracker was a meticulously designed spreadsheet that provided an in-depth analysis of our school's population, categorized by grade level, and systematically tracked daily absences. This organized framework enabled me to present the School Administration Team with detailed attendance rates, expressed as percentages for each grade and for the entire student body, broken down into daily, weekly, and monthly segments. The spreadsheet's advanced features included the ability to identify specific weekdays with notably high absenteeism rates, thereby revealing patterns that could inform targeted interventions. Understanding these dynamics was critical to our efforts to improve our children's daily attendance and foster a culture of consistent classroom engagement.

Furthermore, I was able to categorize each student based on their attendance history—whether they fell into groups reflecting frequent absences or proudly maintained perfect attendance. This granularity not only highlighted the commitment of those with unbroken records but also provided insights that could drive initiatives designed to encourage absentee students to return. The wealth of information captured in this comprehensive spreadsheet transformed raw data into actionable strategies, ultimately aiming to create a more connected and present student community.

The central focus of this model was to classify attendance into two distinct categories: excused or unexcused. By making this crucial distinction, I was better positioned to assess the overall attendance dynamics within the student body. The attendance model provides detailed statistical insights, enabling a clear visualization of the percentage of students within each category. This analysis proves instrumental in identifying areas where additional interventions are necessary, enabling proactive engagement with students experiencing attendance challenges.

In this way, I identified specific students who may benefit from tailored support services designed to improve their attendance. The model serves as a critical resource for ongoing student attendance tracking, enabling swift identification and implementation of effective interventions for students who need extra support. By systematically monitoring attendance patterns, I can spot emerging trends that may indicate deeper issues affecting a student's engagement and overall academic success.

The School Administration Team must be acutely aware of which day of the week has the highest absence rate. Once this information is determined, it can inform the strategic scheduling of school events or programs designed to increase attendance. Understanding where students are at all times is essential for fostering accountability and ensuring effective learning. This begins with intentionality and a continuous commitment to being aware of the school's environment, ensuring that the data remains visible and accessible for ongoing analysis and action.

We are all aware that no student can be absent on the first day of school. It is only after the student shows up for the very first time that the school can start marking the student absent. While students may have registered for classes during the summer or at the time of registration, we face a significant limitation in our attendance procedure. We cannot officially mark a student as absent until we can verify their presence in the building—specifically, until they arrive and occupy a designated seat in the classroom. This policy ensures that schools maintain accurate attendance records.

For example, we have parents who register students during the early registration process. During the summer, the family might move outside the district. The mother registered the student at another school within the district. If you are showing the student as absent, this data is not accurate. What about the students who registered during the registration period but do not show up until after Labor Day? No, you cannot show those students as absent. You cannot show them as present either. You can remove them from the roster if they have not shown up for accountability. I would suggest that those parents be sent to your Student Services office to find out why those children have not been in school. Do not allow parents or guardians to drop off their children at school after the school has been in session for one week or more without a direct conversation with the parent or guardian. Accountability starts the first day. When we begin to hold others accountable at all levels, we start to change the trajectory of the outcomes that will reap dividends later within our school environment.

Let's examine the data charts shown below. The data provide a comprehensive overview of a school population. The accompanying diagrams include a detailed chart that illustrates the attendance data of the collective students. By examining this data closely, we can identify students who might benefit from targeted interventions due to irregular attendance patterns. Additionally, we will highlight students who have achieved perfect attendance, ensuring their names are prominently displayed throughout the school in recognition of their commitment and dedication. We must be strategic in keeping the ideal attendance group of students aware of their accomplishments each day. This is where a kiosk board or poster boards can be utilized throughout the school to celebrate these students. This analysis aims to foster a supportive learning environment while encouraging all students to strive for consistent attendance. The data collection in the diagrams below is hypothetical for each semester. You must understand the shift in the data. The perfect attendance group is getting smaller, while the number of students who need some form of intervention is growing larger. This is where you need to ensure an intervention is put in place for those students. A contract should be the first intervention; an hour-long Attendance Class or Saturday School will assist you in changing the behavior of students who need some intervention to modify their behavior. As we review the charts below, the first semester reflected a healthy school attendance culture. A minimal number of students required some form of intervention. The other diagrams clearly illustrate a concerning trend: student performance has deteriorated each semester. This decline raises significant concerns, particularly given that the data suggest no interventions or support measures were implemented to address these issues. Over time, worsening data points indicate a lack of proactive strategies to improve student outcomes, underscoring a critical need for effective interventions to reverse this trend.

Diagram A

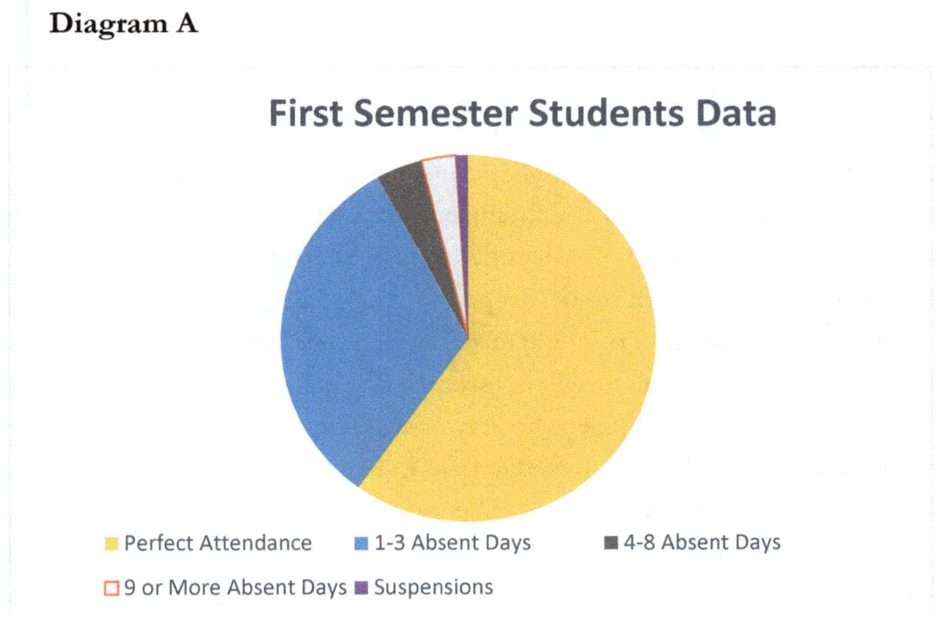

Let's discuss the diagrams.

In Diagram A, 8% of your student population should have an intervention in place to improve their daily attendance. These students fall in the low percentile of your student population. This group of students and a parent or guardian should have met with a counselor or school administrator and had an intervention in place. The school proudly fosters a vibrant culture of attendance, as reflected in first-semester data showing that a significant majority of students are consistently present. However, for those students who accumulate more than three absences, it is essential to implement a structured attendance contract and a tailored intervention plan. This proactive approach allows the school to closely monitor and track each student's attendance behaviors, ensuring they receive the support they need.

To facilitate this process, parents of students with excessive absences must meet with a designated school administrator. During this meeting, they will discuss and sign the attendance contract, which outlines expectations and the specific intervention strategies to be employed.

Furthermore, it is essential to establish clear communication practices; therefore, the school will no longer accept handwritten attendance notes for this group of students. Once an attendance contract and intervention plan are in place, handwritten notes from students or their families to excuse absences should no longer be permitted. This policy aims to create a more accountable and organized approach to attendance, ultimately fostering a better learning environment for all students. It is essential to recognize that students with perfect attendance and those who have missed only a few days of school should continue to be acknowledged by kiosks or an ideal attendance list posted in classrooms, hallways, or the cafeteria so that they can see their accomplishments daily. Keeping these students motivated boosts morale and provides a sense of value daily for those who are making strides to attend school.

Diagram B

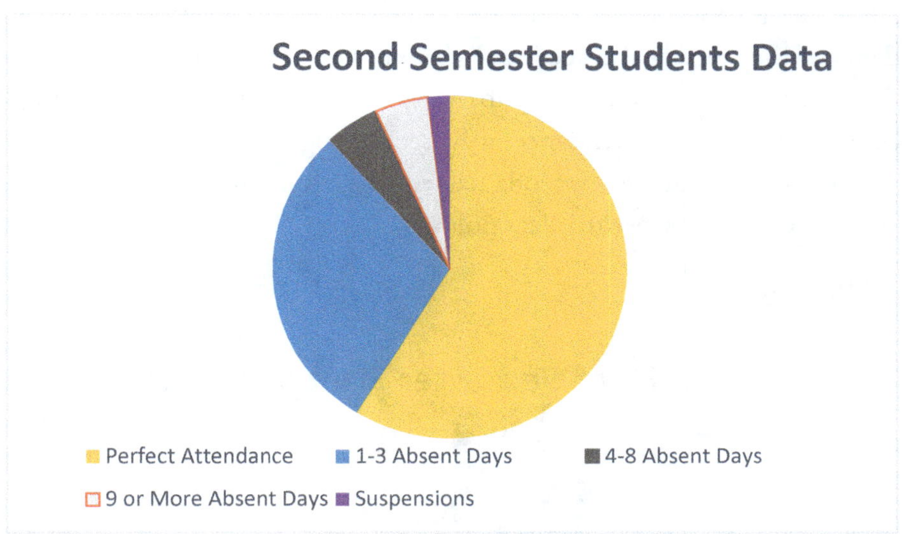

Diagram B illustrates the attendance chart for the second semester. Diagram B reflects that 15% of the student population should have an intervention in place. There is a concerning trend among students with four or more absences. The numbers for these students are increasing, and it is essential to implement a plan of action before their absenteeism significantly impacts the overall daily attendance data. It is crucial to be strategic, as the rising number of students with four or more absences could lead to a detrimental shift in your attendance standards if not addressed promptly. Keep in mind that an absence is an absence, regardless of whether it is classified as excused or unexcused. Each absence carries weight and contributes to one's overall attendance record, reflecting the importance of presence in any setting.

It is essential to recognize and applaud students with perfect attendance while also providing incentives to motivate those who are consistently present. Publicly acknowledging these achievements will have a greater impact on the student body and foster a culture of accountability. It is essential to maintain ongoing communication with the parents of students who provide handwritten notes or, in some cases, no notes at all regarding their absences. Engaging in these discussions will enhance understanding of each student's circumstances and ensure they receive the necessary support while maintaining accountability daily. If interventions regarding absences are not implemented during the specified dates, your attendance will decline significantly. The data from semester 2 shows that while attendance remains strong overall, there have been noticeable changes across the data points.

Diagram C

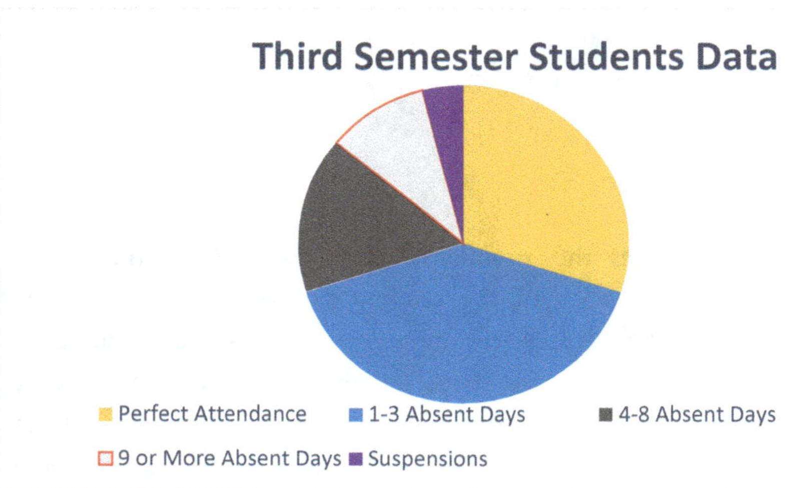

In Diagram C, it is evident that students with four or more absences significantly affect the attendance data. Currently, 16% of the student population has 4-8 absences, and an additional 10% has missed nine or more days of school. This analysis is based on the third-semester data. The third-semester attendance data reflect a notable shift in the attendance culture compared to the first and second semesters. This data reveals that 30% of the student population is still maintaining perfect attendance. Data show that 40% of students have fewer than four days of absence. It is essential to continue recognizing and celebrating these students to sustain this positive trend and ensure the integrity of our attendance data. This shift is particularly pronounced in schools that have been more accepting of handwritten notes as legitimate justifications for absences. When 10% or more of a school's student body is absent for 10 or more days, there is an urgent need to strengthen the attendance culture to foster a supportive environment for all students.

With a typical school year comprising 180 days, missing 18 days or more can significantly hinder a student's academic progress and undermine the overall school environment. Therefore, we must work collectively to implement strategies that not only encourage attendance but also address and support the underlying issues contributing to student absences.

Diagram D

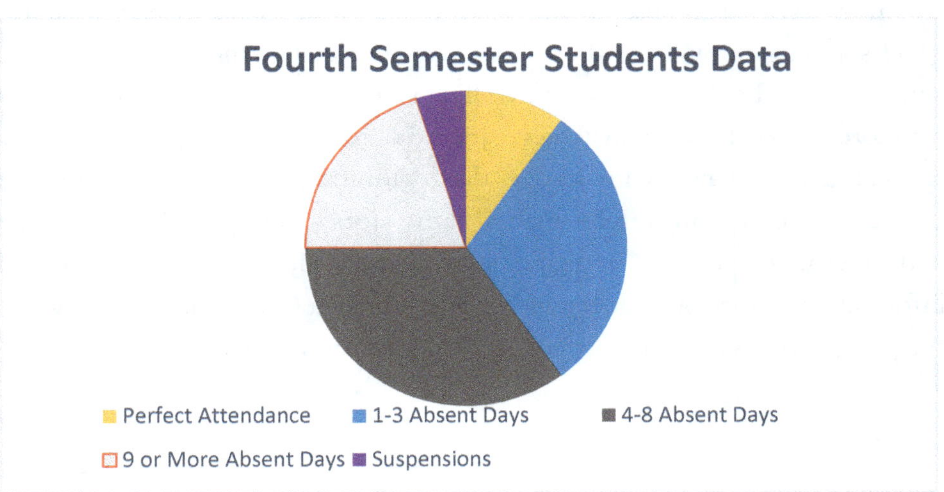

The fourth-semester data show a poor attendance environment. The suspension rate is also a key driver of declining attendance data. The suspension rate for the 4th quarter is 5%. Can we afford to suspend students for every minor infraction? No, not if you want your attendance culture to thrive. We must be strategic! The majority of the school population has missed more than three days of school. Every student, except those with fewer than four absences, should have an intervention in place. Yes, even those who have received a suspension. A contract or intervention between you, the parent, and the student will help build a rapport and create transparency on all levels.

As you begin your analysis of the data diagrams above, it is crucial to identify which student groups within the school fall into each category. Understanding these distinctions will enable you to formulate targeted strategies that improve student attendance. By closely tracking attendance trends and patterns, you can proactively address factors contributing to absenteeism and implement effective interventions. This approach will ultimately help prevent attendance rates from declining to an undesirable level within the school.

It is essential to analyze and monitor your attendance data to maintain good standing throughout the school year. Understanding when attendance shifts occur, why they happen, and which students are involved will help you set more strategic goals and achieve desired outcomes. Every piece of data we encounter weaves its own narrative, filled with insights and implications. It is our responsibility to carefully analyze these stories, interpret their meanings, and determine the most appropriate responses. How we engage with this information shapes our understanding and influences our actions, highlighting the profound connection between data and decision-making.

Chapter 10

Community Partners

All school administration teams actively seek out outstanding community partners who are genuinely invested in their school vision. Such collaborations can yield significant benefits across multiple dimensions, including resource sharing, funding opportunities, and program support. However, it is imperative to assess whether these partnerships are being fully leveraged. Therefore, I encourage you to engage in candid, critical discussions with your community partners by posing the following essential questions:

1. **Funding Commitments:** What is the total amount of funding you can provide to our school in the current academic year? Understanding this helps set clear financial expectations.
2. **Attendance Support:** How much funding can you allocate specifically to initiatives aimed at improving our attendance standards? This is crucial for maintaining student engagement and academic performance.
3. **Connection to Additional Partners:** Are you able to assist us in networking with other community partners who could contribute resources or support throughout the school year? Expanding our network can amplify your impact.
4. **Funding Transparency:** How much funding are you currently receiving specifically on behalf of our school? This transparency will help us grasp the overall financial landscape.
5. **Grant Review:** Could I have a copy of the grant documentation related to the services you intend to provide? This should be readily available for review to ensure accountability.
6. **Allocation Accountability:** Are we receiving all the funding allocated in the grant? It is vital to confirm that the promised resources are actually reaching your students.

73

By asking these questions, you can better understand the resources your community partners can provide. We must remain vigilant to prevent these organizations from exploiting our students. During their visits, partners may overlook pressing issues, yet later submit grant applications claiming they are addressing these very problems, which raises concerns about their commitment to your educational goals.

The school administration should actively begin the search for community partners during the vibrant summer months. By late spring, school leaders will have received vital outcome data from their state's Department of Education, painting a comprehensive picture of the previous year's performance. Once this data has been thoroughly analyzed, it becomes an opportune time to brainstorm and devise innovative strategies for the upcoming school year. During this critical period, it is essential to engage potential donors by inviting them to share their insights and visions, ensuring they feel a part of your school's mission. This collaboration not only enriches your vision but also fosters a sense of community investment in your goals. Take the time to discover their budgetary constraints and the unique resources they can offer to enhance your school or district's programs.

Through this inclusive approach, I have discovered that when everyone has a voice, it leads to fruitful outcomes and strengthens community bonds. Numerous businesses in your community can help create a vital partnership for your school. Discuss with them how crucial it would be for them to invest in your students throughout the school year. Their collaboration will benefit the upcoming school year. When community partners and leaders identify specific needs within a school, they must take proactive steps to address them. For instance, how can leaders from faith-based organizations visit a school lacking necessities—such as functional water fountains or adequate classroom supplies—and overlook these pressing issues? While the phrase "trust the process" is often repeated as a mantra, I firmly believe that our trust should be placed in the realities we observe. We must demand accountability from all stakeholders involved—administrators, community leaders, and policymakers—for the success and overall well-being of our children. Only through active engagement and a commitment to addressing these critical needs can we ensure that every child receives the support and resources they deserve.

When considering potential community members to engage, the church should undoubtedly be at the forefront of your mind. The church can play an invaluable role in supporting your schools and addressing students' needs. We should not have to be members of a particular church to ask for a partnership. Our children are our future. The church should applaud your efforts.

The church can mobilize a network of volunteers to make a significant impact across various aspects of student development. These volunteers can serve as tutors, mentors, or even classroom assistants, offering individualized attention that is often necessary for students who are struggling. For instance, they can work with students who need interventions for attendance, ensuring they understand the importance of being present in class and helping them overcome any barriers they may have. By meeting weekly with these students, volunteers can provide ongoing encouragement and support, helping them develop better habits and stay on track academically.

Moreover, volunteers can assist with core subjects such as reading and math, collaborating with teachers to reinforce the curriculum and address knowledge gaps. Their involvement can help create a more supportive and engaging learning environment, ultimately improving student outcomes. By establishing collaborative relationships between schools and community partners, such as churches, we can foster a network of support that enhances our children's educational experiences and prepares them for future success.

Our community partners have untapped potential to support and enhance the student population beyond mentoring relationships. Not all partners need to give monetary resources. A few partners can provide items that can serve as student incentives. For example, I had a music store provide me with several pieces of equipment that I put in place for students in music who needed some accountability for their daily attendance. The students were excited about working toward winning one of the items donated by the music store.

Many businesses in your community can serve as valuable sources of support, including banks, beauty salons, barber shops, non-profits, colleges, and dental offices. Don't hesitate to seek assistance from these local businesses. For instance, some banks across the country participate in the "Pay for Grades Initiative," which offers monetary stipends to students who achieve A's or B's on their report cards. This initiative can be a great motivator for our students. If the banks in your community are not part of this program, consider proposing it to establish a beneficial partnership. Not only can this initiative encourage our children to excel academically, but it can also promote regular attendance and student accountability. If a bank declines to participate in the "Pay for Grades Initiative," ask what other support they might be willing to provide for your school or district.

I highlighted the importance of collaborating with barbershops and beauty salons because I encountered many students who were hesitant to attend school because their hair was not properly groomed. Establishing partnerships with local hair care professionals allows us to offer certificates for services such as haircuts, roller sets, and cornrows. These services can make a considerable difference in encouraging students to take pride in their appearance and to attend school regularly. Furthermore, we can use these certificates as tools to promote accountability among students and their families regarding personal hygiene. Once we determine that a student's absenteeism is related to hygiene issues, we can provide these certificates directly to their parents. This approach not only addresses the immediate problem of absenteeism but also fosters a culture of self-care and responsibility within the community.

Pediatric dental offices can not only provide financial support to your school but also offer free cleanings to your student population. Those businesses that provide services to our children are more than willing to assist schools in your community with the support needed for our children to succeed. If there are universities or colleges in your area, it can reap dividends if you get with the dean of students to see if a partnership can be put in place with those college students whose majors are teaching, counseling, etc. Students can participate in enriching internships at your school, contributing valuable hours each week in exchange for academic credit. These dedicated individuals can serve as tutors or mentors, providing much-needed support and guidance to fellow students who may be struggling. Their involvement not only enhances their own learning experience but also fosters a collaborative and supportive educational environment for everyone.

The movie theaters located in your city can offer complimentary passes each semester to students who demonstrate consistent improvement in their daily attendance records. These passes serve as a reward for dedication and commitment, encouraging students to maintain regular attendance and stay engaged in their studies. By recognizing and celebrating student achievements, the theaters not only promote a culture of responsibility but also offer students an enjoyable opportunity to relax and unwind with a film of their choice. Bowling alleys and skating rinks are additional businesses that can provide passes each semester. These passes can serve as excellent incentives for your students. Having a non-profit organization as a partner can provide funding, mentors, and additional resources.

Let's discuss how partnering with a non-profit organization can provide funding, mentors, and an array of resources. Non-profit organizations play a crucial role in supporting educational institutions by providing a wide range of services beyond academic assistance. They can offer valuable mentoring programs that foster personal and academic growth among students, often pairing them with experienced mentors who can guide and encourage them throughout their educational journeys.

Additionally, these organizations may offer financial aid opportunities specifically designed for high school students, helping them to afford necessary resources such as tuition, textbooks, and college application fees. I worked at a non-profit that provided laptops to high school graduates preparing for college. Furthermore, non-profits are instrumental in addressing the fundamental needs of children and families, including access to food, clothing, and housing support, ensuring that every student has the essential tools to succeed both in and out of the classroom. Many non-profit organizations can serve as bridges between home and school. The heartbeat of a non-profit organization is crucial for schools that struggle to meet the many challenges they face involving students and families. Learning how to incorporate these partnerships into your schools or district is vital to their lasting success.

Lastly, you can write a proposal for your school attendance initiative. The proposal may be sent to ten or more local businesses in your area. The proposal should reflect what your requests are for your school or district. When requesting donations, it's essential to clearly explain how the funds will benefit your students. Based on my experience, a school with a student population of 500 or fewer would significantly benefit from a $750 donation to implement attendance incentives. For a school district with 5,000 students or fewer, a $2,500 donation would be substantial for using attendance incentives. In a school district with up to 10,000 students, a $5,000 donation would be impactful. It is crucial to be strategic in determining where and how these incentives are implemented to support student growth effectively.

There are numerous opportunities and strategies available to secure resources for your attendance initiative. To begin, it's essential to start with a clear vision of your end goals. Always keep in mind the partners who have generously invested in your children's education and well-being throughout the school year. You can extend invitations to them for your end-of-year celebrations, where you can acknowledge their support with personalized certificates presented during the ceremonies. This not only honors their contributions but also strengthens your relationship with them.

Furthermore, consider creating thoughtful thank-you cards that your students can sign. This personal touch allows the students to express their gratitude directly, making the gesture even more meaningful. Regardless of a partner's age or achievements, everyone appreciates the simple yet profound act of taking the time to say, "Thank you." Recognizing your partners' contributions fosters a culture of appreciation and encourages continued support for your initiatives.

You have already made significant progress in this process. It's now essential to identify and engage potential partners who can help you achieve your objectives and positively transform attendance outcomes for your students. Think about organizations, community leaders, and educational institutions that share your vision and can provide valuable resources, expertise, or support. Collaborating with the right partners will be crucial in implementing effective strategies and ensuring sustained improvement in student attendance.

Chapter 11

Get Ready, Get Set, Let's Go!

We are at the end, but just beginning a journey on behalf of our students. Trust everyone on your team to be on deck. I would love to receive information regarding the success of your end-of-year celebrations. Trust me, it will work! I suggest inviting a former student each year to address the student body on the importance of attending school. Do not lose hope! Remember, you will have some resistance, but it will not last long. Change is hard for those whom we are trying to support. I applaud all of you for your dedication to our children. Please do not forget, you are changing lives, and this takes a lot of determination, grit, and motivation. You are not alone! This journey will yield numerous rewards. I can promise you that your outcomes will be greater and your students will reach higher heights because of your efforts.

How can you get started? First, by realizing that our children enjoy a challenge. In your district, you can have all elementary schools compete against each other each semester or annually. The elementary school with the highest attendance percentage for the semester can win a dance or a pizza party. If you do not want to compete as a district, you can have your students compete within their classrooms within your school. The key factor is what will keep your students engaged and motivated to attend school throughout the school year.

I have noticed that middle and high school students demonstrate a strong desire to compete for individual prizes, which can significantly enhance their motivation and engagement. To capitalize on this, we could organize an attendance drawing each semester, offering appealing items such as a tablet or an iPad. These devices are available at reasonable prices from an online retailer, making them a cost-effective incentive. Furthermore, bicycles serve as another exciting attendance incentive that our younger students are particularly enthusiastic about winning. You could order a selection of colorful bikes and prominently display them on the cafeteria stage, ensuring they catch students' attention each time they enter the building. This visual reminder can serve to inspire students to maintain consistent attendance.

I would recommend assigning a staff member to create and oversee the attendance initiative within your school. This person should work to generate excitement and promote fairness in raising awareness about students' daily attendance. It's essential that this individual closely monitor daily attendance for all students. The attendance awards should be presented during the Semester Award Ceremony. The names of the perfect attendance students should be drawn publicly during the event, promoting transparency and adding an element of anticipation. This approach will not only celebrate those with perfect attendance but also encourage students who may not have achieved it to strive for better attendance in the future. By implementing these strategies, we can foster a more positive school culture that values commitment and rewards effort.

Announce the attendance incentives to your students on the first day of school to set a positive tone for the year. To maintain motivation, integrate these incentives into your daily announcements throughout the week, emphasizing their importance in fostering a culture of attendance. Create a visually engaging bulletin board in a high-traffic area of the school that prominently displays the daily attendance rate. In addition, feature students with perfect attendance in a designated section to acknowledge their commitment and serve as role models for their peers. This will not only celebrate individual achievements but also provide a strong encouragement for other students to prioritize their attendance.

Consider offering specific rewards or recognition for consistent attendance, such as monthly or semester prizes and certificates, as well as during special events, to further motivate students. It's essential to make these rewards meaningful to your school's mission and to ensure they stand out clearly, thereby creating a vibrant environment where attendance is recognized as a valued aspect of student success.

You are now poised to effectively implement your strategic attendance plan for your school or district, setting the stage for increased engagement and improved outcomes. I have placed a few survey questions below to show you how to effectively start a conversation about getting your students and parents engaged in the importance of attending school. These questions can break the tension before implementing an intervention for a student. These questions provide the parent an opportunity to share their views concerning why the student might be absent from school. These are only a few questions you can use to get the answers you are seeking from a student or parent. Make your surveys intentional.

I believe you are ready to set the standards for your students to grow and for your attendance outcomes to match your investment.

STUDENTS' ATTENDANCE QUESTIONNAIRE

NAME: ______________________________GRADE: ____________________

1. Share with me something that you find important about yourself.
2. Do you believe that attending school every day is important? Why or why not?
3. What is your favorite subject in school, and why do you enjoy it?
4. Is there a subject that you find challenging? If so, what steps are you taking to overcome this challenge?
5. If you enjoy team sports, tell me what your favorite team sport is and why you like it.
6. Are you a member of any sports team in your school? If yes, which team and what do you enjoy about being on the team?
7. How many athletes from your state have become professional athletes in the sport you enjoy? How does that make you feel about your potential as an athlete?
8. What is your dream job, and how will attending school every day help you achieve it?
9. Explain your plan for achieving your dream job.
10. How many school days have you missed this year? Do you believe that these absences have affected your learning?
11. How many days do you think you will miss this school year? What steps can you take to ensure that you are present for every school day?
12. What is the reason for your absences from school? Can anything be done to reduce these absences?
13. Have you ever had perfect attendance for a semester? If yes, how did it make you feel, and did your school acknowledge your achievement?

14. Have you ever had perfect attendance for the entire school year? If yes, how did it make you feel, and did your school acknowledge your achievement?
15. In your opinion, what is an acceptable number of days for a student to miss from school? Explain why you think this number is appropriate.
16. What motivates you to attend school every day? Is there anything that could increase your motivation?
17. When you are absent from school, what steps do you take to ensure you do not fall behind in your studies?

Middle and high school students:
18. Write a five-paragraph essay on the importance of attending school daily. Consider the impact that regular attendance has on academic success, social development, and future career opportunities.
19. What subject do you prefer during morning classes, and why?
20. Can you please explain if you believe that attending school every day is crucial for future success?
21. Please describe how you feel about your role as a student and its significance in your school environment.
22. Would anyone in your school environment notice or tell you that you were missed during the period of your absence? If so, who?

Thank you for taking the time to complete this survey. Your responses will help us to better understand how to support your academic success.

PARENTS' ATTENDANCE QUESTIONNAIRE

STUDENT'S NAME: _______________________

STUDENT'S GRADE: _______________

1. Parents or guardians, please write five sentences that describe your child. No more than five sentences.
2. Does your child enjoy attending school? Please explain.
3. What are your child's strengths as it relates to their academic success?
4. What would you say is a challenge for your child as it relates to their academic success?
5. Has your child shared their aspirations for after high school with you?
6. Do you have a support group to help your child academically? If not, would you like additional support from school staff? Please explain.
7. How can the school support your child's success?

Thank you for taking the time to complete this survey. Your responses will help us better understand how to support your child's academic success.

References

Chan, Edward, Mentoring Paradigms: Reflections on Mentoring, Leadership, and Discipleship

Covey, Stephen M. R. The Speed of Trust

Gordana, S., The Ultimate Guide to Shaping School Culture, 2020

LOVE   Respect   Hope

Susie Winfield

About The Author

Susie Winfield believes in divine guidance. She is an Army veteran, a retired police officer, and is certified in Urban Ministry. She holds a Bachelor of Science degree in Organizational Management. Susie has dedicated a significant part of her career to helping the thousands of students and families who face challenges with consistent school attendance. With over 30 years of mentoring experience, she has worked closely with families and students, gaining valuable insights into the barriers to regular attendance. This book aims to highlight innovative and strategic methods she has utilized throughout her career, designed to inspire and motivate children to value their education and attend school consistently.

This book is dedicated to Susie's grandchildren, Jeremiah and Kinsley, as well as to all school-age children, to help them understand the importance of attending school each day. It is dedicated to all school staff members who provide vital support and guidance to our children. This manuscript reflects the author's commitment to nurturing the next generation. Through heartfelt stories, practical solutions, and expert advice, readers will discover the tools they need to foster a positive attitude toward attending school and learning among their students.

Susie also expresses her gratitude to her wonderful husband, Steven, for his unwavering support throughout the development of this resource, as well as to those who contributed by proofreading or offering feedback.

www.ingramcontent.com/pod-product-compliance
Lightning Source LLC
Chambersburg PA
CBHW061749050726
47598CB00002B/659